Peeking at Pillars

(quotes on quotes on writing)

Steven R. Lundin

Acknowledgement: Thank you to all of those listed in Appendix B for assembling writing quotations and making them available on the public domain. You inspire writing.

Photographs of pillars, fountain, and stepping stones by Steven Lundin.

ISBN: 1470034077
ISBN-13: 9781470034078

DEDICATION

For Pago, Play, and Pilch

STEVEN R. LUNDIN

ACKNOWLEDGMENTS

This book is the result of Becky's encouragement,
Pauline's laughter, and Lisa's love. Thank you, thank
you, and thank you.

CONTENTS

FOREWORD

I was between novels when I read my first writing quotation, but I was so taken by the words, so enchanted by the wisdom, and so drawn to finding universal truths about writing, that I spent the following year collecting, reading, and writing about writing quotations. I must have read thousands of them. I went from nodding, laughing, and enjoying these treasures of truth to questioning and commenting on what the pillars of literature were saying about writing. In this manner—by peeking at pillars—I saw universal reflections of the human experience.

In the pages that follow, you will be looking at life through the eyes of writers—peeking around their psyches—and by doing so, you will catch glimpses of yourself. I know I did.

The format of each quotation is as follows: I precede each quotation with a title, place the quotation and source in *italic* print, and then add a short comment expanding the meaning.

Peeking at Pillars is for readers and writers, men and women, young and old, and the busy and the bored. I intend its bite sized portions will make it ideal for travel or late night reading.

STEVEN R. LUNDIN

1 | ON HOW TO WRITE

Allow Writing

"If I don't write to empty my mind, I go mad."
   - Lord Byron

Every time I feel like I'm going mad trying to empty my mind, I stop writing. I've learned that writing is not something to force. It's something to allow.

Insomnia

"The only cure for writer's block is insomnia."
   - Merit Antares

Another quotation about writer's block? Really? Shhh. Let's be quiet so those writers who still believe writer's block is real can keep sleeping. We insomniacs will keep on writing.

Hook of the Bottle

"If your vision of a writer involves sitting in a cafe, sipping an aperitif with one's fellow geniuses, become a drunk. It's easier and far less exhausting."
  - William Hefferman

Writers drawn to the lure of image are easily caught by the hook of the bottle.

Just Call it Fiction

"The best way to become acquainted with a subject is to write a book about it."
  - Benjamin Disraeli (1804-1881)

Writing a book is also a great way to expose the gaps in writers' knowledge of a subject. It is when they find these holes that they face the important decision: Conduct research or not? It turns out Disraeli's quotation works for both answers. Writers who conduct research do become acquainted with their subjects, but so do writers who fill the voids with imagination. They simply call their work fiction, just like their research.

Siphoning Words

"Writing comes more easily if you have something to say."
  - Sholem Asch

When writers have something to say, their words gush like water from a dam. The writer's challenge is to turn the knob, stop the flow, and sponge the spill. Writing with nothing to say is like siphoning sand through a hose. The writer sucks, spits, and sucks, and so does his writing.

Curse a Bit

"I just sit at my typewriter and curse a bit."
  - P. G. Wodehouse

Replacing spools and threading new ribbons, positioning paper, untangling type bar jams after typing too fast, slamming the carriage at the end of each line, using your weakest fingers to shift the carriage and make capital letters, hearing the mechanical thuds -- or silence -- of your thoughts, and erasing raw wounds onto paper, painting letters with globs of whiteout, or simply pulling paper out of the roller like rye in a wheat field, crumpling them, and throwing the wads on the floor near your basket. I would cuss too. Today's writers are fortunate to have computers. That is, they're fortunate when the damn things work.

Short Things

"Good things, when short, are twice as good."
  - Baltasar Gracián

So true.

Why Write

"There are many reasons why novelists write — but they all have one thing in common: a need to create an alternative world."
  - John Fowles

I have trouble with writing quotations when powerful beginnings are followed by weak opinions -- opinions I do not, cannot, and will not share. Is it true? Is "a need to create an alternative world" the "in common" reason novelists write? Really? "[T]he need to create an alternative world" is more consequence than reason. Novelists write because they love writing. Now there is a reason!

Ending Again

"Great is the art of beginning, but greater is the art of ending."
  - Longfellow

Greatest of all is ending again, and again, and again...

One Quote a Day

One quote a day keeps writing in play.
  - S.R. Lundin

Had to be There

"Writing well means never having to say, 'I guess you had to be there.'"
  - Jef Mallett

Well written means being able to say, "I felt I was there."

The End

"Advice to writers: Sometimes you just have to stop writing. Even before you begin."
  - Stanislaw J. Lec

Instead of stopping before you begin, get started and quit at "The End."

Roaches

Writing errors are like roaches. If you find one, you can be sure hundreds more lie hidden in your manuscript.
  - S.R. Lundin

Drunk on Writing

"You must stay drunk on writing so reality cannot destroy you."
  - Ray Bradbury

This is yet another quotation that causes me to nod my head and think, "I know what you mean." Rather than drunk, though, where the writer staggers from sentence to sentence, his fat tongue slurring his paper voice so that readers smell in their minds what they read on his pages, and hearing and smelling a drunk, they toss the work, the writer needs only nips from the writing flask. He needs them every day. The liquor of writing, like that of the bottle, can destroy the writer, but when taken in nips, it loosens the writing tongue. Then can he talk!

Resource for Affluent Writing

"If you have other things in your life -- family, friends, good productive day work -- these can interact with your writing and the sum will be all the richer."
  - David Brin

Ahh, yes-the other things in life. Writing a novel is like taking a daily journey to some foreign land, where you visit new sites, meet new people, learn their language, and get so involved in their lives that you start knowing what they know, wanting what they want, feeling what they feel, and fearing what they fear. Leave them and go to work. Spend time with your friends and family, mow the lawn, throw a stick to the dog, and pay your bills. Affluent writing comes from lives rich with experience. David Brin is right: these other things are the resource for affluent writing.

Climax of Inspiration

"You can't wait for inspiration. You have to go after it with a club."

- Jack London

If I had waited for inspiration before pursuing my desire to write, I would still be journaling little nothings. Jack London was right about going after inspiration. He said writers should use a club, but I think they should use a finger. Instead of beating inspiration into submission, writers should caress it like a love. Press it. Fondle it. Inflame such a passion for writing that they reach the climax of inspiration. After that, write. Do it again and again, but writers beware. Inspiration carries a big club.

Stab of Rejection

"Engrave this in your brain: EVERY WRITER GETS REJECTED. You will be no different."
  - John Scalzi

Engraving the words in your brain hurts like the prick of a piercing, but it's nothing compared to the first stab of rejection.

Know and Feel

"It's better to write about things you feel than about things you know about."
  - L. P. Hartley

Know what you feel, feel what you know, and write who you are.

Two Parts Decision

Recipe for Writer's block: One part enthusiasm, two parts decision, and three parts procrastination.
  - S.R. Lundin

Seat of Your Feet

"The art of writing is the art of applying the seat of the pants to the seat of the chair."
  - Mary Heaton Vorse

Writing quotations reveal writers. While most writers understand and share certain truths about writing--like the need to write every day--some come up with clever little thoughts that I do not share. Apply the seat of the pants to the seat of the chair? That's funny, but it's also irrelevant. I write on my feet.

My son built a stand-up desk for me after I complained that chair writing was taking my strength. With muscles, it's use them or lose them and, after only four years of writing every day, sitting for hours in front of a keyboard, out of the elements, indoors, warm, soft, and sedate, I discovered chair writing is unhealthy writing. Maybe it would be different if I could still run. Between writing, I would go out, get my legs working, arms pumping, lungs gasping, and blood gushing. That would be something! Then I could safely sit for hours and write. I could laugh out loud at Mary Heaton Vorse's little quotation.

As it is, I adapted her words to my situation. The art of writing, then, is the art of applying the seat of the feet to the head of the floor.

Scrubbing the Basement

"Rewriting is like scrubbing the basement floor with a toothbrush."
  - Pete Murphy

I happened across this quotation at an unfortunate time in my life. I had challenged myself to write an entire novel in quotation marks (by having a character tell the whole story, just like Joseph Conrad had Marlow do in "Lord Jim") but, as soon as I completed the first draft of the book, I awoke to the truth that readers no longer care for the mental price it costs them to read such a work.

I was told today's readers prefer entertainment --I call it mindrest word watching. As a consequence, I rewrote the entire book, and that is when I read Pete Murphy's quotation. I remember frowning, stopping what I was doing at the time, nodding my head in agreement, spreading my arms in submission, and speaking out loud at my desk.

"Damn right, Murphy! Where were you forty days ago?"

A Professional Writer

"The only reason for being a professional writer is that you just can't help it. "
  - Leo Rosten

As long as I do not have to write every day, I will write every day. Does that mean I will never be a professional writer? Oh well.

The Unconscious

"The story arises in the unconscious."
  - Dorothea Brande

Just after finishing high school, I read a book by Dr. Maxwell Maltz explaining how the unconscious mind serves as what he called a "servo-mechanism." I cannot remember why I read such a book, especially as it was not assigned by a teacher, but I can remember what I learned. When we sleep, our minds do not.

Dr. Maltz claimed the mind uses the down time to process the problems, challenges, and concerns of the conscious day. That is why, he explained, there are so many students, scientists, musicians, researchers, and business men and women who wake up knowing answers to their questions, inventing something from nothing, or simply discovering something amazing. The subconscious mind finds answers in the night. The moment I read Dorthea Brande's quotation about writing, I though of Dr. Maltz and his idea of the mind accepting input during the conscious day, processing it during the unconscious night, and producing output in the morning. It works for writers! Writers do not need to be concerned about their stories. All they have to do is sit down and write. Even if the first day ends in frustration, the outcome is good for the process. What is on the mind is in the mind.

Before starting my first novel, I was entirely uncertain about what I would write. I knew only that I had to write to become a writer. Everything from settings and scenes to characters and themes developed along the way. The subconscious fine tuned my story, plot points, the growth of my protagonist, decline of the antagonist, and everything else that went in the writing. The point? Don't wait. Just write. Let your mind figure it all out for you.

Create Your Taste

"Every great and original writer, in proportion as he is great or original, must himself create the taste by which he is to be relished."

- Samuel Taylor Coleridge

What truth! There are thousands, maybe millions, of writers whose published works were good in their day. Maybe they wrote romance novels or westerns, science fiction, historicals, or some other of those genres found on bookstore shelves. Many of these books can be found using Wikipedia, Google, or smashed on a shelf in a public library. The works of relished authors, on the other hand, are leather-bound, spine-stamped with real gold, gilded, printed on archival quality paper, stitched with satin bookmarks, and found in the libraries of private collectors, in bookstores, airports, vacation resorts, and certainly in neighborhood libraries; they last. What separates the good from the great?

Arguing in favor of one reason is like arguing in favor of one temperature over another. Some like hot and others like cold. The reason is found with great and original (GO) writers. GO writers do more than entertain their contemporaries. They birth ideas that affect the human condition. I remain impressed by the foresight of Adulous Huxley in his Brave New World, but my favorite example is Harriett Beecher Stowe with her Uncle Tom's Cabin. She wrote more than a story. Because she was brave and original so was her work. When President Abraham Lincoln met Stowe in 1862, he is said to have remarked, "So you're the little woman who wrote the book that started this great war!"

Of course, books don't start wars. Men do. President Lincoln was simply making Coleridge's point.

Falsies and Gummers

"Writers like teeth are divided into incisors and grinders."
  - Walter Bagehot

What of the others, the falsies and the gummers? While false teeth writers can be quite clever, gummers can only gnaw on your patience like a newborn gumming your finger. She gnaws, sucks, and slobbers but never takes a bite. A writer bites and leaves a mark.

From the Soul

"Write from the soul."
  - Jefferey A. Carver

Wallet writers write for money. They have a knack for getting both your attention and your money without ever revealing their souls. Soul writers, on the other hand, have a knack for revealing their souls first and then losing both your attention and your money.

Writing Survives

"Success comes to a writer as a rule, so gradually that it is always something of a shock to him to look back and realize the heights to which he has climbed."
  - P.G. Wodehouse

Put a frog in a pan of cold water, turn on the heat, and watch what happens. When the temperature rises as slowly as success comes to a writer, the frog boils to death without feeling it happen.

Writers have the opposite problem; they do
not feel cold. Encourage them to publish and watch
what happens. When the temperature lowers as fast as
rejection comes to writers, they freeze without feeling it
happen.

While frogs boil and writers freeze, writing survives.

Life Side of Hell

Writing without passion is torture on the life-side of hell. If it's
your job, then it's only hell on earth.
  - S.R. Lundin

The Public Purse

"The public is the only critic whose opinion is worth anything at
all."
  - Mark Twain

Just follow the money. The public criticizes with a
purse.

Fighting Rewrite

"There is no great writing, only great rewriting."
  - Justice Brandeis

Sure, I took him on. He was just so damn cocky, and I, well, I had just finished my first novel, *Shooting an Albatross*. I was not about to stand by and let him taunt me.

"My writing's fine the way it is," I challenged.

"All you've done," Rewrite said, nodding his head, curling his upper lip, and turning his head as though dismissing my work, "is nothing. Anyone could do what you did. You wrote a story. So what? That's it. It's not a great writing. You know what you have to do now. Let me hear you say it? Let me hear you say my name. Rewrite. Rewrite, Rewrite."

"You'll see."

"Bring it," Rewrite countered, whispering, grinning, and touching his gloves to mine.

In the twelfth round of our fight, Rewrite began landing the words of Justice Brandis' quotation in a combination of short little jabs that snapped my head left and then right. He stayed on me the entire round. It was jab, snap, "There is no great writing, only great rewriting," jab, snap, "There is no great writing, only great rewriting," jab, snap, "There is no great writing, only great rewriting."

"Rewrite!" the crowd yelled and then turned its yell into a chant. "Rewrite! Rewrite! Rewrite."

I staggered backward until the give in the ropes stopped giving, and it was there that I made my final stand. I switched from a left- to a right-hand lead, hoisted the thick manuscript I had worked so hard to write, and used it as a shield against Rewrite's press.

'Your writing is great the way it is.' The thought came from somewhere deep in my mind. Was it pride speaking to me? 'You wrote a beginning, a middle, and an end. The great work is done. You don't need to rewrite it. Your writing is great the way it is.'

Rewrite stood in front of me, trapping me against the ropes, and throwing a combination that connected with my plot, uppercut my dialog, found and exposed a weakness in the development of my characters, and he then lowered his aim to deliver a series of body shots that made the sound of a baseball bat hitting a pumpkin. He was relentless. He kept swinging, and I kept trying to block the blows by turning my manuscript to the left and the right. He was just too fast. My head snapped left then right. My mouthpiece flew off to the ground, the pages of my manuscript fell like leaves in the fall, and the pages landed on top of the spatters of my blood and sweat that were everywhere down on the canvas.

What happened? I know I'm lying flat on my back, where I keep my eyes closed and hear the roar of the crowd like it was the sound of the ocean. I hear the referee counting, too, and his interval numbers sound to me like the waves in a set.

"Eight, nine, ten," he yells. "Rewrite is winner by knockout!" The announcer speaks with the voice of Justice Brandeis.

I turn and look to where I find Rewrite standing and looking at me from the far side of the ring. He is holding his hands in the air and smiling at me. I see my manuscript scattered everywhere on the canvas between us, so I climb to my knees crawl about the floor, sweeping the floor with my arms and collecting the pages of my manuscript like they were cards from a deck. I pin the disheveled papers against my body with my left hand, aim the pointer finger of my right hand at Rewrite, spit blood, and yell.

"I want a rematch!"

"As soon as you rewrite," he says.

2 | ENCOURAGEMENT FOR WRITERS

The Itch of literature

"When once the itch of literature comes over a man, nothing can cure it but the scratching of a pen."
   - Samuel Lover

The scratch of a pen, pound on a ribbon, and tap of the keyboard are nothing more than sounds. It is the writing that relieves.

The Author as a Mother

"An author who speaks about his own books is almost as bad as a mother who talks about her own children."
  - Benjamin Disraeli

The comparison of an author with a mother, where one births a book and the other a child, where both invest their every emotion into what one day leaves them wondering at home, is as common as the sentence. The simile is a metaphor. Sure the two can, will, and do talk about their creations without cease, but just go ask anyone who has created anything. You will hear the exact same bias, favor, and enthusiasm that you hear coming from the author and the mother. The truth is, creators love their creations.

What a Writer Wants

"What a writer wants to do is not what he does."
  - Jorge Luis Borges

This quotation is frustrating. Writers want to write, but they get so involved in the publishing and promotion of their work that their writing time shrinks from pages to paragraphs. Foremost, writers do what they have to do so they can someday do what they want to do. But isn't that true for everyone?

Bore the Reader

"It is a cardinal sin to bore the reader."
  - Larry Niven

Whether it is the whisper of a nudge, shout of a shove, or scream of a scratch, published authors can always hear the sound of their success or failure. Unfortunately, it can happen after they have already lost their readers, and to get them back requires something like forgiving a cardinal sin. It takes a miracle. It takes a savior - just don't go there.

Don't Quote Me

Screenplay writing is more like computer programming than real writing, but don't quote me on that.
  - S.R. Lundin

Good for the Wealth

"Writing is hard work and bad for the health."
  - E B White

Writing is bad for the health but good for the wealth, excluding money of course.

Nail Biting

"Work every day. No matter what has happened the day or night before. Get up and bite on the nail."
  - Ernest Hemingway

Hemingway's advice is great. Try it. Get up and write every day -- no matter what you did the night before or at what time you went to bed. And don't worry about biting the nail. In time, you'll feel like you've swallowed it whole.

Hopelessly Sane

"It is rarely that you see an American writer who is not hopelessly sane."
  - Margaret Anderson

You see the crazy ones everywhere.

Wait

"I don't wait for moods. You accomplish nothing if you do that. Your mind must know it has got to get down to work."
  - Pearl S. Buck

Waiting to write, whether on mood, money, or inspiration, is waiting for nothing, for nothing always comes.

Grammar Rejected

If text and texted, but flex and not flexted, then grammar rejected.
  - S.R. Lundin

Presence is Absence

"Writing is a struggle between presence and absence."
  - Lu Ji

While writing, presence is absence.

When Writing

Feeling the emotions of your characters is as natural as laughing when you're happy or crying when you're sad.
  - S.R. Lundin

Writing is to Reading

Writing is to reading what cooking is to eating.
  - S.R. Lundin

What Your Hero Wants

"First, find out what your hero wants, and then just follow him!"
- Ray Bradbury

How simple! Just find out what your hero wants and follow him. The problem I have with Bradbury's clever simplification is the fault of my hero. He, she, or it is dynamic; he grows with the story. When I give my hero a bicycle, he wants a cell phone. As soon as I give him a cell phone, he wants a car. A car becomes money, an education, job, spouse, house, stuff, and little heros of his own. I can barely keep up with him! A restated version of Bradbury's quotation that works for me is: decide what your hero needs and lead him to it.

The Antonym of Dictionary

"A synonym is a word you use when you can't spell the other one."
- Baltasar Gracián

A thesaurus is full of words you should never use. I use mine as the antonym of my dictionary.

The Writing Ride

"The faster I write the better my output. If I'm going slow I'm in trouble. It means I'm pushing the word instead of being pulled by them."
   - Raymond Chandler

Back when I was writing my first novel, there were mornings I wrote two, four, and six thousand words. The words flew from my fingers. I also had mornings where I wrote a single page, one paragraph, or that one time when I managed just a sentence - one sentence! I was in trouble that morning.

The secret when writing goes slow is to keep writing. Don't quit. If you keep pushing your words, they eventually crest whatever peak is slowing you, and then they will fly down the other side and take you with them. That's when you get to hang on and enjoy the writing ride.

Live

"The most solid advice...for a writer is this. I think: Try to learn to breathe deeply, really to taste food when you eat, and when you sleep, really to sleep. Try as much as possible to be wholly alive, with all your might, and when you laugh, laugh like
   - William Saroyan

William Saroyan's advice is quite good. He brings to mind Thoreau's "How vain it is to sit down and write when you have not stood up to live." Unfortunately, he also brings to mind F. Scott Fitzgerald's "First you take a drink ... then the drink takes you." Writers beware that you are not so busy breathing, eating, sleeping, living, laughing, and getting angry that you never get around to writing. That is how the living takes you.

The Muddle

"Many modern novels have a beginning, a muddle and an end."
   - Philip Larkin

Character is in the muddle.

Write in the Zone

"The strokes of the pen need deliberation as much as the sword needs swiftness."
   - Julia Ward Howe

Professional basketball players "in the zone" do not deliberate. Their years of dedication, passion, and practice gives them the stroke and swiftness of a champion. They seem "unconscious" while they are playing. The same can be true for writers. Beginning writers should, and do, over think their words, sentences, and paragraphs, remembering to dribble first, thinking to plant their foot, to box-out, rebound, keep their hands up, and so on. They practice for years. While only a few ever write in the zone, most writers are satisfied just being unconscious.

Anger Writes Noise

Words sound the emotions of your moments. When you're angry, never write about love. Anger writes noise. Instead of weakness, write out of your strength. When you are happy, the mood spreads through your writings like sunlight through the dark, touching, lighting, and warming even the coldest pains of your heart. Happiness writes itself.

   - S.R. Lundin

Live with That

"Life cannot defeat a writer who is in love with writing; for life itself is a writer's love until death."

   - Edna Ferber

Even though I believe writing will be my love until death, I wonder. If life cannot defeat a writer, why is it beating the hell out of me? Apparently, I have writing to thank for my survival; I'll just have to live with it.

Writing Straight Out

"I know that if I have been working on one paragraph and I have written it three times, it goes in the bin. Unless it comes straight out, it is wrong, it is awkward, it does not fit."

   - Robert Rankin

Forcing sentences and paragraphs makes writing hard work. Easy writing is easy work. Robert Rankin says it well: Writing is right, comfortable, and fits when "it comes straight out."

A Writer Tries

"A man in public life expects to be sneered at—it is the fault of his elevated situation, and not of himself."
- Charles Dickens

Writers expect to be rejected, if not the fault of their writing, it's the fault of their trying to do what others will not.

Rushed Writing

Rushed writing is slow work.
- S.R. Lundin

Failure Lacks Endurance

Keep writing. Failure lacks endurance.
- S.R. Lundin

Screenplay to Movie

Screenplay is to movie what grin is to smile.
- S.R. Lundin

Writing Day

"Being a real writer means being able to do the work on a bad day."
   - Norman Mailer

When every day is a writing day, everyday is a good day.

Enough Rope to Hang

"I would never write about anyone who is not at the end of his rope."
   - Stanley Elkin

Instead of the end of their ropes, write about characters with enough rope to hang themselves. It raises the stakes, ups the tension, tingles the spine, and turns the page.

Do it in Private

"Writing is not necessarily something to be ashamed of, but do it in private and wash your hands afterwards."
   - Robert Heinlein

One time, when I was working on my first novel, I went to a coffee shop and wrote in public. Writing was still new to me; I didn't know what I didn't know. So I go to this place, sit with latte and laptop, and enter the fictitious world of my story, where my hero had goals, obstacles to overcome to achieve those goals, a love interest, an antagonist with competing goals, and a character arc that was only half of a rainbow. As I got into the story, I got out of the present. I saw the story as it unfolded in my mind, grinning through one whole scene, smiling at a twist in plot, raising my arms in wonder, laughing out loud at the irony, and stopping only once to have a drink of the latte. The cup was full. The drink was cold.

In their furtive glances, I realized that the people in the coffee shop were thinking what Robert Heinlein said in his quotation. "[Write] in private." As for washing my hands afterwards? Let's just say I write in a much cleaner genre.

Idiots, Fools, and Buffoons

"In certain kinds of writing, particularly in art criticism and literary criticism, it is normal to come across long passages which are almost completely lacking in meaning."
  - George Orwell

All writers, after encountering such passages and trying to understand them, uncovering their flaws, raging against the stupidity, and then coming to some final place of piece -- if such a place exists -- should consider the critic behind the criticism.

It helps when creating believable characters who are idiots, fools, and buffoons.

Surviving Interruptions

"The process of writing has something infinite about it. Even though it is interrupted each night, it is one single notation."
  - Elias Canetti

Writing is life's ultimate interruption.

Droplet of Wisdom

"Metaphors have a way of holding the most truth in the least space."
  - Orson Scott Card

A droplet of wisdom.

Accidental Plagiarism

"I write for the same reason I breathe - because if I didn't, I would die."
  - Isaac Asimov

The moment I read Asimov's quotation, I took a gasp of breath and stabbed my mouse pointer on a Web link titled "Author's Den." The author photograph of me sitting on my porch swing appeared, and I saw next to the photograph the words I sought. I read the short quotation I had written to describe myself: "I could no easier stop writing than I could stop breathing." I took a moment to compare the two quotations, Asimov's and mine, and I dismissed my concern for having committed accidental plagiarism. A court would rule Asimov's stated reason for writing was to prevent his death, whereas the same court would conclude my reason for writing was simply to continue breathing. Because life-support systems could keep me alive, it could be argued, I could stop writing, stop breathing, and live.

I would get off on a technicality!

To the thousands of others who equate their writing to their being alive, good luck. I recommend you go after a class action dismissal of our class action passion.

Barf of Words

"I have made this [letter] longer, because I have not had the time to make it shorter."
  - Blaise Pascal

Every first draft barf of words needs cleaning. Whether the mess forms a note, letter, story, or novel, it remains a puddle on paper until the author cleans it up with rewriting. The work stinks, seems as though it will never end, and takes more than too much time, but it is by dirtying their hands they make their work shine. What Pascal did was clever. He just scented his letter with the perfume of a disclaimer and then went on with his day.

32

The Hardest Work in the World

"Writing is the hardest work in the world. I have been a bricklayer and a truck driver, and I tell you -- as if you haven't been told a million times already -- that writing is harder. Lonelier. And nobler and more enriching."

- Harlan Ellison

The demands of life far exceed every difficulty with writing. They are like hyenas, one pulling a leg, another tugging a mouthful of hair, a third clenched at the throat, some number behind where they can be heard and felt, and then there's that snarling and snapping one coming straight for the belly. What is writing? Sitting, thinking, creating, feeling, and typing? How nice. I wish I had the time. It sounds so easy, but what do I know? I would name my hyenas if it wasn't so damn hard to write.

Prove Your Talent

"Writing is an occupation in which you have to keep proving your talent to those who have none."

- Jules Renard

Writers must prove their talent first to themselves and then to agents, publishers, marketers, advertisers, publicists, distributors, wholesalers, retailers, reviewers, critics, news men and women, and everyone else with a voice of rejection, to say nothing of their families and friends. Fortunately, most aspiring writers never get past themselves.

Characteristic of You

*"The characteristic of Chaucer is intensity: of Spencer, remoteness:
of Milton elevation and of Shakespeare everything."*
    - William Hazlitt

... the characteristics of you, who knows? Write
something. Let posterity figure you out.

Answer with a Letter

*"What a lot we lost when we stopped writing letters. You can't
reread a phone call."*
    - Liz Carpenter

What's worse? Being unable to reread a phone call or
not being able to read all of your email? Answer with a
letter.

Day is Done

*"To withdraw myself from myself has ever been my sole, my entire,
my sincere motive in scribbling at all."*
    - Lord Byron

Writers cannot withdraw themselves from their
writings. It doesn't work. Sure we might read a story in
which the characters, action, and dialog captivate us for
three hundred pages or more, but then we are done.
Whether in genre, voice, grammar, punctuation, or
style, the writer is there in his story, and then there's the
cover. Go to any bookstore and look at the bestsellers.
Most titles are small compared to the names of their

authors. Today, Lord Byron's quotation is long out of date; it reads like he wrote it when the earth was still flat. Byron was a poet and, in his defense, readers seek themselves in poetry instead of the poet. In books they seek the story, and that is where they always find the writer. Poets withdraw and writers advance.

Splatter Write

"Creativity is allowing yourself to make mistakes. Art is knowing which ones to keep."
  - Scott Adams

Splatter words on a page and call it art? No thanks. Prepare with a bucket, write with a bucket, edit with a brush.

End of Editing

"The best time for planning a book is when you're doing the dishes."
  - Agatha Christie

When you're outside, the best place for planning a book is the seat of a mower.

The Three Rules for Writing a Novel

"There are three rules for writing a novel. Unfortunately, no one knows what they are."
  - W. Somerset Maugham

The rules for writing are the same as those for living with MS. Sufferers must make own rules, and those with MS must do the same.

3 | THE SILLY AND THE SERIOUS

Rite Right Wrong Write

Rite Right? Wrong Write.
  - S.R. Lundin

Once Upon a Time

"May I never grow too old to treasure 'once upon a time'."
  - Anonymous

May I remain young enough to write it.

The Only Way to Learn

"The only way to learn to write is to write. "
  - Peggy Teeters

Many quotations about writing lack only the child's belch of "duh."

Truth Inside the Lie

"Fiction is a lie, and good fiction is the truth inside the lie."
  - Stephen King

Calling fiction a lie is like calling a romance a porno, but Stephen King gets away with the belch by identifying good fiction as the truth inside a lie. The thought is magical and yet, bad fiction is not a lie around the truth, like the peel around an apple. Bad fiction is rotten clean to the core.

Whisper Write

"What I like in a good author is not what he says, but what he whispers."
  - Logan Pearsall Smith (Afterthoughts)

Reading is like listening to your father. When he talks, you listen. When he shouts, you miss most of what he says. When he preaches, you think of your plans for later that night, and when he whispers, you never miss a word. Writers must use every voice if their whispers are to scream.

Victory for Life

"Every word written is a victory against death."
  - Michel Butor

Every book written is a victory for life.

Years Yet to Live

"For your born writer, nothing is so healing as the realization that he has come upon the right word."
  - Catherine Drinker Bowen

For your dead writer, nothing is more discouraging than the realization he has years yet to live.

Take out the Trash

"It is perfectly okay to write garbage--as long as you edit brilliantly."
  - C. J. Cherryh

Anyone who has rummaged through a bag of garbage, looking for receipts, packaging, or maybe a rebate coupon they tossed by mistake, knows what it's like to finger an awful mess of coffee grounds, plate scrapings, meat wrappings, and the like. The work stinks, but so does editing a manuscript. Anyone can write garbage, but they are great writers who learn to take out their trash.

Whisper in the Library

"Hard writing is like yelling in a nursing home. Easy writing is like whispering in a library."
  - S.R. Lundin

The simple truth.

Totter like the Rest of Us

"The act of putting pen to paper encourages pause for thought, this in turn makes us think more deeply about life, which helps us regain our equilibrium."
  - Norbet Platt

This is comforting for new authors. Out there is balance. Get up. Keep writing, especially after the effort to become a writer knocks the crap out of you. Until you regain your equilibrium, keep going; all you have to do is think shallow and totter like the rest of us.

Relief of Silence

"Writing is a struggle against silence."
  - Carlos Fuentes

On the contrary, writing is relief from the noise of characters, stories, themes, plots, and ideas all clamoring for attention. Writing is a relief of silence.

Exquisite Burden

"Revision is one of the exquisite pleasures of writing."
  - Bernard Malamud

Had Bernard Malamud called revision one of the "necessary burdens" instead of "exquisite pleasures" of writing, I would think of him like a brother. Instead, he's more the father my mother left before I was born.

Face of Writer's Block

"A blank piece of paper is God's way of telling us how hard it is to be God."
  - Sidney Sheldon

If God speaks to us through blank pages, then blank computer documents are His way of telling us to write. If not, they're Satan's way of scaring us with writer's block.

Celebrate Writing

"Forget all the rules. Forget about being published. Write for yourself and celebrate writing."
  - Melinda Haynes

Remember the rules. Think about being published. Write for everyone and wait to have your big party. That's how you celebrate writing

Foundation of Frustration

"The road to ignorance is paved with good editors."
  - George Bernard Shaw

The library of writing quotations has a foundation of frustration.

Antagonism Acts with Reason

"Heroism feels and never reasons, and therefore is always right."
  - Ralph Waldo Emerson

Antagonism feels and acts with reason, and therefore is always wrong.

Legless

"A critic is a legless man who teaches running."
  - Anonymous

Worse is the crowd that runs with him.

Damn Hard Writing

"Easy reading is damn hard writing."
  - Nathaniel Hawthorne

He says it well. However, I have never met anyone who says Hawthorne is easy reading. Rather, they complain about his dated use of the English language. His words sound in the mind like a preacher's but, from my experience raising three young adults, I know

Hawthorne still manages to capture attention with his compelling stories. They laughed where Hawthorne would have them laughing, complained where he would have them complaining, and followed to where he led their minds. He was an excellent writer.

Be Readable

"The virtue of books is to be readable."
  - Ralph Waldo Emerson

Writers should write with Emerson's words in mind. If not, then they write for themselves, probably quite well, too, but their work will more likely reside in journals kept under their desks than on book shelves in stores. Some say that money is not the object, and I agree. Writing is the point, but for whom do we write? Readers.

Create a universe, populate it, add a protagonist, confront him or her with an antagonist, give them opposing goals, stir the pages with conflict, and make your readers demand to read a next page. Just watch what happens.

You can have everything you want. Why? Because "[t]he virtue of books is to be readable." Emerson was right.

A Labour to Write

"A bad book is as much of a labour to write as a good one; it comes as sincerely from the author's soul."
  - Aldous Huxley

I have been to several "pitch" conferences where authors pitch their books to literary agents. Their goal is to secure agent representation. Some authors leave smiling, most leave wondering, a few get angry, and one or two always go away crying. Their souls are in their works, as Huxley observes, as sincerely as their labor. How could it be otherwise? Who could perform such a labor as writing a book without committing the full of his or her soul?

Unfortunately, Huxley's purpose was less obvious than his point.

Play as Deep as Calculus

"The pen is the tongue of the mind."
  - Miguel de Cervantes

I read Cervantes' Don Quixote as an undergraduate in my final year of college, at a time I was taking advanced calculus, a tough course of mathematical proofs. I used Cervantes as a counterbalance to the rigors of proving calculus.

On the math side of the balance, I had to prove everything: this from that, that from this, this and that from that and this, and so on. On the other side of balance, there was Don Quixote. What nonsense! Cervantes' main character named himself Don Quixote de la Mancha, dressed in an old coat of armor, mounted an old nag he also burdened with armor, rode with a lance, and went off on a series of knightly adventures that were as ridiculous as calculus was rigorous.

Cervantes said, "The pen is the tongue of the mind," but I hold that the tongue is the tongue of the mind. Because his barefaced humor helped me to conquer advanced calculus, I now accept Cervantes pen above my tongue.

The point? I asked that same question after finishing the novel. My answer was that numbers and words mix in the mind like oil and water. Once mixed and shaken, though, like salad dressing in a bottle, the two become one, but I am still searching for an Einstein to explain the mixture.

It was Cervantes who taught me to have fun when mixing both parts, and he did so while making a point in his novel nearly as complex as calculus.

Hemingway's Iceberg

"If a writer of prose knows enough about what he is writing about he may omit things that he knows-- and the reader, if the writer is writing truly enough, will have a feeling of those things as strongly as though the writer had stated them. The dignity of movement of an iceberg is due to only one-eighth of it being above water."
- Ernest Hemingway

I wrote Shooting an Albatross in three sections. The titles of the sections come from the game of golf, where a player begins by driving his golf ball off of a tee, next hitting the ball down a fairway, and finally putting the ball until it falls in a hole in the green. I named these sections "The Drive" (introduce the characters, their goals, the historical setting, and so on), "The Fairway" (develop characters, important relationships, and competing goals), and "The Hole" (where the story turns into somewhat of a psychological thriller). I show pieces of ice here and there but, by the time readers reach "The Hole," they know that each chunk of ice was the tip of an iceberg. Hemingway's icebergs are helpful for showing just enough, causing readers to wonder, and surprising them with what lies under.

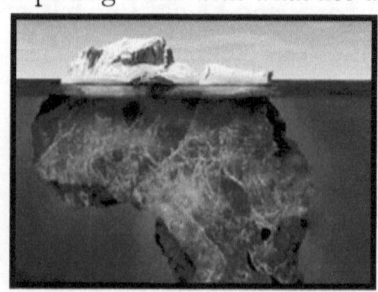

Dream of Perfection

"The work never matches the dream of perfection the artist has to start with."
   - William Faulkner

What Faulkner calls the dream of perfection is, like nectar, nip, or pollen, an elixir that keeps artists trying for the perfection they see in their minds. It intoxicates them. They see the beautiful, try for it, and present it to the world when the two match close enough. It's never perfect, though, for today's artists must be pragmatic. It is the reason they can accept the little imperfections of their work.

Hear, Feel, and See

"My task...is to make you hear, to make you feel--and, above all, to make you see. That is all, and it is everything."
   - Joseph Conrad

Doctor, make you hear,
Preacher, make you feel,
Teacher, make you see
Writer? ... make you hear, feel, and see?

"That is all, and it is everything."   - J. C.

4 | WARNINGS ABOUT WRITING

Just Aim

"Unless one is a genius, it is best to aim at being intelligible."
- Anthony Hope Hawkins

Genius is intelligible. Rather than aim to emulate, aim to exceed. Let history say where you miss.

The Truth about Authors

"A good novel tells us the truth about it's hero; but a bad novel tells us the truth about its author."
  - Gilbert K. Chesterton

I was once concerned that readers would see me in my writings. If I described a tree, they would think it was the one in my yard. If I wrote about an idiot, they would accuse me of making fun of an acquaintance. If I described a pretty woman, then I must be attracted to so-and-so. The beginner thinks Jr. High thoughts.

The truth is that readers get so involved in good books that the author ceases to exist. Authors of bad books, ironically, cease to exist too.

Two Kinds of Writer

"There are two kinds of writer: those that make you think and those that make you wonder."
  - Brian Adiss

The writer who spends time wondering what his readers think has way too much time on his hands. He's either already published his novel or he never will.

Finished

"I just wrote a book, but don't go out and buy it yet, because I don't think it's finished yet."
  - Lawrence Welk

Like most everything written for laughs, the words of this quotation expose a truth that I find disturbing at some deep level. I have written a book. It's finished, and now it is selling on the Internet, but I cannot read it without wanting to change this, tweak that, reinsert the one chapter I removed from the book, or change a thousand little nothings. A writer could spend his whole life trying to perfect his one book.

Books are finished the moment they get published, but so too are most writers.

Excellent Writers

"Only a mediocre writer is always at his best."
  - Maugham, W. Somerset

The opposite of this quotation is absurd: An excellent writer is never at his worst. All you have to do is interrupt an excellent writer while he is writing and see what happens.

Interrupt a mediocre writer and he'll see you.

Failure Gone Green

"A ratio of failures is built into the process of writing. The wastebasket has evolved for a reason."
  - Margaret Atwood

Failure has evolved. From write, wad, and toss, it has become key press, backspace-backspace, delete-delete-delete, cut, copy, and paste. Failure has gone green.

When a Nation Loses

"If a nation loses its [writers], it loses its childhood."
  - Peter Handke

When a nation loses its readers, it loses its wisdom.

Will and Desire

"I see the notion of talent as quite irrelevant. I see instead perseverance, application, industry, assiduity, will, will, will, desire, desire, desire."
  - Gordon Lish

If you write until you feel Lish's meaning, you will never stop.

Authors and Lovers

"Authors and Lovers always suffer some infatuation, from which only absence can set them free."
  - Samuel Johnson

Check that; it's absence, not abstinence.

Favorite Book

If you have a favorite book, then you haven't read enough books.
  - S.R. Lundin

Great Effort

"When something can be read without effort, great effort has gone into its writing."
  - Enrique Jardiel Poncela

When something can be written without effort, great effort is needed to proof it.

Rejection

"Rejection slips, or form letters, however tactfully phrased, are lacerations of the soul, if not quite inventions of the devil - but there is no way around them."
  - Isaac Asimov

No trying, no rejection. One rejection, one broken heart. One hundred rejections, one hardened heart. Years of rejection, one hell of a writer.

Inspired Writing

"Good work doesn't happen with inspiration. It comes with constant, often tedious and deliberate effort."
  - William Hefferman

Inspiration is what makes the "constant, tedious, and deliberate effort" to write as easy as breathing, addicting as living, and pleasurable as... well, as pleasurable as whatever you enjoy the most. Inspired writing is no work at all.

Focus

"Words are a lens to focus one's mind."
  - Ayn Rand

Focus on words, see the sentence, Focus on sentences; see the paragraph, Focus on paragraphs, miss the story. Focus small; write big.

One Reason

"Getting even is one reason for writing."
  - William Gass

...Like getting drunk is one reason for drinking. Despite the reason you pull the cork from a bottle, you drink. Despite the reason you put words down on paper, you write, and that is enough.

Mastery

"Few men make themselves masters of the things they write or speak."
  - Tirso de Molina

Masters do not write today and not tomorrow. They commit their lives to "mak[ing] themselves masters." Passion and commitment are just fundamentals. Discipline is their high truth.

Resolve to Write

New year, new story: Write every day. By this time next year, you will either be filled with the passion or emptied of the dream.
  - S.R. Lundin

Window to the Author

Story is a window to its author, like shoes are a window to his wallet.
  - S.R. Lundin

Write, Lead, and Follow

Write so men might read; lead so they might follow; follow so they will write.
  - S.R. Lundin

All That You Want

"Most of the shadows of this life are caused by our standing in our own sunshine."
  - Ralph Waldo Emerson

Read more than you write, learn more than you know, then write all that you want.

How to Become A Writer

"It is by sitting down to write every morning that one becomes a writer."
  - Gerald Brenan

Most people understand the concept of the average as something that represents the middle of a collection, like the average of a collection of numbers, scores on a test, traveling speeds, and so on. Average is intuitive, but the related words mean, median, and mode are less so, and they inspire not understanding nods but blank stares, like the stares beginning writers make as they wonder how to become real writers.

Fortunately, the answer is found in the averages -- the mean, median, and mode -- of the collections of quotations about writers and writing. All three equal the center, most common, and most repeated answer: Write every day. The time of day matters less than the frequency, but I appreciate Gerald Brenan's little addition about writing every morning. Writers are wise to fit writing ahead of the concerns of their day. If not in the morning, they should write at mid-morning, noon, afternoon, evening, night, or up to and past midnight.

You become what you do.

Mistake of the Unknown Author

"A metaphor is like a simile."
  - Author Unknown

Mathematical Proof:

Given two variables X and Y, we say:

      [A] Metaphor: X is Y
      [B] Simile: X is like Y

Subtract: [C] = A – B
             = Metaphor – Simile
             = (X is Y) - (X is like Y)
             = (X-X) + (Y-Y) + (is-is) – like
             = -like

Unknown Author's law: [D] = Metaphor = like Simile

Substitute [D] into [C]: Metaphor – Simile = -like
                          like Simile – Simile = -like
                                 like = -like
                                (FALSE!)

Therefore: A Metaphor is not like a Simile

Alternate: Metaphors and Similes are like way cool

Pleased with the Bad

"People do not deserve to have good writing, they are so pleased with bad."
  - Ralph Waldo Emerson

New writers should read these words with caution, to resist the lure of excuse and to avoid blaming the rejection of their work on the poor taste of readers. Readers will read both good and bad writings. The trick for new writers is to make theirs better than the best or worse than the worst.

If it's bad enough, the worst is called the best.

But Writing?

"Planning to write is not writing.
Outlining…researching…talking to people about what you're doing, none of that is writing. Writing is writing."
  - E.L. Doctorow

"You're doing exactly what you want to do."

"No I'm not."

"Sure you are. If you were not doing what you want to do, then you would do something else."

"What I want to do is write. I plan to write a book someday so, you see, I'm not at all doing what I want to do."

"When you really want to write, you will make room in your life for writing. You are not writing now because you are doing something else. You are doing what you want to do."

"No I'm not."

"Sure you are."

"But I have bills to pay, a house to maintain, kids to raise, a lawn to mow, and that damn barbecue this weekend."

"Those are the things you want to do"

"No. Those are the things I have to do."

"Same thing. You do what you have to do so you can have what you want to have. You want the things that brought those bills? You want the house, cars, kids, lawn, and time with the friends coming for the barbecue?"

"Sure I do."

"And that is why you are doing exactly what you want to do. When you really want something else, you will do whatever it takes to get it."

"But writing?"

"That is what you might do. When I see you writing, you will be doing what you say you want to do. Until then, you are not writing."

"But I'm doing what I want to do."

"That's what I said."

The Great and the Poor

"Great writers begin as great readers but so do poor writers. The difficulty comes when trying to distinguish the two. The great think they are poor, and the poor think they are great."
  - S.R. Lundin

Art of Words

"Literature is all, or mostly, about sex."
  - Anthony Burgess

Literature is not at all about sex. If it was, then more people would write, but fewer would read. Literature is, instead, the art of words, painted with fingers and viewed in minds.

Lovers Siblings and Enemies

"Ink and paper are sometimes passionate lovers, oftentimes brother and sister, and occasionally mortal enemies."
  - Emme Woodhull-Bäche

The relationships between ink and paper are the same relationships writers have with their writings. When writing, they have passionate lovers. When editing, siblings, and when they get stuck waiting for inspiration, they have mortal enemies. How ironic it is that only their mortal enemies cannot kill them.

Their lovers and siblings are another story.

Hell on Earth

"My working habits are simple: long periods of thinking, short periods of writing."
   - *Anonymous*

Imagine the opposite working habits: short periods of thinking and long periods of writing. If not dystopia, the opposite would be the writer's hell on earth.

Fiction's Spider

"Fiction is like a spider's web, attached ever so slightly perhaps, but still attached to life at all four corners."
   - *Virginia Woolf*

Fiction's spider plays. She abandons her web the moment she senses the writer's approach, enticing him to explore her sticky trap. And then she returns, then she bites. Instead of devouring him, though, she leaves him stuck on a one genre web. She knows from experience that most writers never escape. Fewer still even try.

Something to Say

"The reason one writes isn't the fact he wants to say something. He writes because he has something to say."
   - *F. Scott Fitzgerald*

Everyone has a story to tell. Most tell it with email, instant messaging, cell phones, chat rooms, social networking, or chewing lips. Writers say it with silence.

Pains of Birth

"When a woman is speaking to you, listen to what she says with her eyes."
- Victor Hugo

Unlike babies, writers must learn to see before they are ready for birth. That is the reason they spend so much time crying about critics, agents, rejection, writer's block, "conspirac[ies] against their talent," having to work so damn hard, and on-and-on. They are seeing and feeling pains of birth.

Transgendered Words Plus Some

"I never knew what was meant by choice of words. It was one word or none."
- Robert Frost

The fashion today is to dress nouns as verbs, verbs as adjectives, adjectives as nouns, and so on. Right words do exist, but they are no longer gender-specific. "[O]ne word or none?" Today, its transgendered words plus some. If you can think it you can use it.

The Best Writing

Writer's Reality: Your best writing is yet to come.
- S.R. Lundin

Freedom

"Writing free verse is like playing tennis with the net down."
  - Robert Frost

I played tennis without a net in Carpentaria, California. It was fun for about two minutes, but then it became a big waste of time. The challenge was to remain interested -- to keep at an activity that required no skill, lacked reward, and offered little more than pseudo exercise. Robert Frost compared writing free verse with playing tennis without a net, but the similarity is limited to a lack of confinement, not enjoyment, improvement, or time well spent.

Exercise Imagination

"Imagination grows by exercise, and contrary to popular belief, is more powerful in the mature than in the young."
  - William Somerset Maugham

Like imagination, ambition weakens without exercise and, in agreement with experience, both are more active in the young than in the mature.

There is your reason -- Exercise imagination now!

Einstein the Comedian

"Imagination is more important than knowledge. Knowledge is limited. Imagination encircles the world."
  - Albert Einstein

Humor is a well known marker of intelligence, and Einstein's humor was some of the best. Knowledge is finite? That's hilarious. After all, knowledge is the seed of imagination--limit one and limit the other.

From Novel to Screen

Going from novel to screen requires a thousand decisions about what to cut and what to keep. Thankfully, the answer to one simple question helps every time: Does it (the scene) forward the story? Yes? Keep it. No? kill it. Not sure? Cut it. When you master the movement of story you reduce adapting to a problem of time. Unfortunately, no one has a solution for time.
  - S.R. Lundin

Afford Poverty

"As a younger man I wrote for eight years without ever earning a nickel which is a long apprenticeship, but in that time I learned a lot about my trade."
  - James Michener

No longer young, in my fifth year of writing, learning the trade, and earning just above a nickel, I advise aspiring writers to start young -- while they can afford poverty.

Sin not Read

"When I am dead, I hope it may be said: 'His sins were scarlet, but his books were read.'"
- Hilaire Belloc

...and still to this day I hear his voice in my head.

A Lifetime of Homework

"Being a writer is like having homework every night for the rest of your life."
   - Lawrence Kasdan

Lawrence Kasdan's quotation means something similar to everyone who reads and laughs at his words. Homework for the rest of your life? Really? Homework like when we were back in school?

Kusdan equated a writing life to a life of torture, but I suspect he did so with a twist on his lip. The truth is that being a writer is like having something you cannot wait to do, every minute of every day, every day of every year, and every year for the rest of your life.

Without pleasure

"What is written without effort is in general read without pleasure."
   - Samuel Johnson

But what is written with great effort might also be read without pleasure. The secret is not in the effort. It is found in the pleasure novelists give to and take from their writings.

A good writer feels like his readers.

A Writer's Discovery

"Writing became such a process of discovery that I couldn't wait to get to work in the morning: I wanted to know what I was going to say."
   - Sharon O'Brien

It happened to me when I was about four chapters into my first novel. The routine of getting out of bed every day to write at 4:00 a.m. had already become my habit. I had gone months without fumbling with my alarm clock, hitting its snooze button, or craving just five more minutes of warm blanket rest. All I wanted in the morning was to get up and write. The sound of my alarm became more the shot of a starter's gun.

Every day was the same. I woke, went downstairs in the dark, made a French press of coffee, started a fire, sat where I wrote, and rejoined my characters right where I left them the previous morning. Had I read Sharon O'Brien's quotation back then, I might have been prepared when it happened to me. I started waking up before my alarm. At first it was 3:45, then it was 3:30, and eight or nine times I actually woke up at two in the morning. Waking was subconscious. I could not wait to get back to work so I could discover where the story would go, what the characters would do, what they thought, and like O'Brien, what they would say.

Every word became a revelation, and paragraph-by-page, writing became that "process of discovery." How strange it is for a writer to say that he could not put down his book, especially when the work had yet to be finished.

I learned that writing is a dual process of discovery. While finding out what they will say, writers discover truths about themselves.

It's no wonder I woke out of wonder.

The Genre of the Ridiculous

"The story…must be a conflict, and specifically, a conflict between the forces of good and evil within a single person."
  - Maxwell Anderson

Question: What happens when the single person is a spider, lion, pig, horse, dog, fish, or tea cup that a writer gave human faculties? Answer: Whatever the writer wants to have happen. Imaginations can go wild in the genre of the ridiculous, but the same can be said about all of the other genres of fiction.

An Excellent Rewriter

"I'm not a very good writer, but I'm an excellent rewriter."
  - James Michener

The word, rewriter, is only one of the thousands of synonyms for writer. If you place the adjective, excellent, in front of any of the other synonyms, you will find that today's quotation still works for James Michener. Despite what he said, he was an excellent writer.

1,000 Story Ideas

"Everybody walks past a thousand story ideas every day. The good writers are the ones who see five or six of them. Most people don't see any."
 - Orson Scott Card

Writers who believe in writer's block, like those who believe in the Loch Ness Monster, a second gunman on the grassy knoll, the Bermuda Triangle, JFK's involvement in Marilyn Monroe's death, or some other decided belief, should carry a note card with Orson Scott Card's quotation written on both sides of it. They should also swipe a yellow highlighter across the word "thousand." Then, with card in hand and mind on the prowl, they will see their first story idea can be about their decision against writer's block.

The Basic Laws of Writing

"Books aren't written - they're rewritten. Including your own. It is one of the hardest things to accept, especially after the seventh rewrite hasn't quite done it."
 - Michael Crichton

One of the hardest things for me to accept is the feeling that I understand and relate to successful, contemporary writers like Mr. Crichton. Arrogant souls presume knowledge beyond their experiences but, after four years, two novels, a stack of short stories, and reading what seems like two thousand quotations about writing, I suspect that authors do share an understanding of some basic laws of writing:

1) writers write
2) writing is hard
3) every write needs a rewrite
4) every rewrite needs another
5) writers are finished once they stop writing (triple meaning).

So what if I recognize and identify with Michael Crichton's mention of the 4th law of writing? That does not make me arrogant. Make-up my own laws of writing? Now that would be arrogant.

Microscope of the Moment

"Never write about a place until you're away from it, because that gives you perspective."
  - Ernest Hemingway

Those writing about a place they are visiting write in the moment. You ride the bus into town for dinner and feel amazed by the wild ride through narrow streets, so cobbled and rough that the windows rattle like rocks falling on rocks, with the doors wide open, the driver going faster than is safe and squeezing the bus to fit it between a confusion of dented buses that look as packed full of natives as your bus, feeling your wife squeezing your knee, daughter squeezing your hand with her little white fingers, and seeing your son gawking and grinning at every site -- shops without doors, signs written in a language he does not understand, tourists waiving their hands to negotiate paying nothing for nothing, twinkle lights on the doors and windows of restaurants, adults wearing shorts and flip-flops, and tourists in hats speaking a pseudo language to which the natives only smile, nod, and never answer. It is a mistake to write what you see through your microscope of the moment. Wait.

Instead, capture everything in your mind and enjoy the experience. When you get home, you will discover that Hemingway was right. Time gives perspective.

Writers need to write with perspective. Instead of a wild bus ride with the natives, you will discover that you rode with commuters going to and from work, sitting in silence, making quiet eye contact with each other, trying to ignore the happy family that stared at them like they were strangely inhuman, and making furrowed glances that you never quite met -- except for the few who lifted their lips after you caught them with your smile – and then you can wonder what you missed behind your back.

In the moment, you see what you feel but, with perspective, you feel what you saw.

Change Yourself

"Everyone thinks of changing the world, but no one thinks of changing himself."
   - Leo Tolstoy

Beginning writers should think of nothing more than writing. Get up, sit down, and write. Imagine, experiment, experience, and learn. They cannot possibly anticipate the challenges they will face. There will come a morning, however, when they wake up to discover that writing has changed everything, in both themselves and in the world. More than ever, that is when they will need to think.

Crazy

"Reality leaves a lot to the imagination."
   - John Lennon

While imagination without reality is only insanity, reality without imagination is death. Writers imagine between insanity and death. They're crazy.

Some Things Never Change

"Not every story has explosions and car chases. That's why they have nudity and espionage."
   - Bill Barnes and Gene Ambaum

Nudity and espionage are cheap easy tricks for getting attention. So, too, are explosions and car chases. But stories in which nothing explodes, where cars stay still, characters remain clothed, and no one spies on their neighbors are boring to modern readers. Ironically, writers today must show meaning in speeding, sneaking, lurking, smashing, and stripping characters. But that's writing. Some things never change.

Objective Confusion

"Objective journalism and an opinion column are about as similar as the Bible and Playboy magazine."
  - Walter Cronkite

I'm confused: Is objective journalism similar to the Bible or to Playboy magazine? I thought objective journalism was cliché for oxymoron. Go figure.

Architecture of Movies

"Prose is architecture, not interior decoration."
  - Ernest Hemingway

Screenplays are the architecture of movies.

Baby Pictures

Seeing your first screenplay is like seeing baby pictures of you in a diaper.
  - S.R. Lundin

Failed Writers

"Some editors are failed writers, but so are most writers."
  - T.S. Eliot

T.S. Eliot may or may not have added that most writers are failed editors. Had he done so, I might have hung a portrait of Eliot over my dinner table. I actually tried to edit my own work, but the story I saw in my mind prevented me from seeing the words on the page. Two two words would sit next to each other, but I could not even see them. Punctuation became unimportant? tense got lost to time, spelling became whatever it was, and every attempt I made to edit my own writing became just another reason to rework the story, theme, plot, character development, and on-an-on. The quotation, both his way and mine (writers are failed editors), explains Eliot's preference for poetry.

True When You Start

"Writers are not just people who sit down and write. They hazard themselves. Every time you compose a book your composition of yourself is at stake."
  - E.L. Doctorow

There's no doubt about it: Writing changes everyone, especially the writer.

Welcome

Hello? Can you hear me? Is anyone there?
  - S.R. Lundin

The question is: can I hear you? and the answer is
no. I cannot. Regardless, welcome to my blog. The
purpose of this blog is to keep my mind engaged with
the matter of writing during this new season for me.
What season is this?   The publishing season. It is
because I am publishing my first novel that I have no
time to write my third novel. Yet, that is exactly what I
want to do. This Blog is the consequence. I am writing
a Blog based on my reactions to quotations about
writers and writing. What will I learn?

5 | TRUTHS

No Hell for Authors

"There is probably no hell for authors in the next world -- they suffer so much from critics and publishers in this."
    - C. N. Bovee

The true wisdom of C.N. Bovee comes from his excluding literary agents from his list of named hellions. Why state the obvious?

Know What You've Stepped In

"The most essential gift for a good writer is a built-in shock-proof shit-detector"
  - Ernest Hemingway

The ear and the tongue are two pieces of the built-in equipment Hemingway elevates to necessities for good writers. Writers should read their work out loud. What they hear with their ears they can taste on their tongues. Still, when their words both sound right and taste good, writers should look down at their shoes.

Good writers know what they've stepped in.

Antidote to Writer's Block

"The best antidote to writer's block is ... to write."
  - Henriette Anne Klauser

What is this writer's block? I heard it described as something that writers in California made-up while sitting barefoot on the beach, looking through shades, swirling ice in their drinks, and searching for inspiration in the fit, tan, and wet-oiled bodies that passed where they sat.

It's not a secret, the antidote to writer's block is not in a bikini.

Your Place in the Grave

"Happy families are all alike; every unhappy family is unhappy in its own way."
  - Leo Tolstoy, Anna Karenina, Chapter 1, first line

Beware the first line in your book. It can preserve your place in history as easily as your spot in the grave.

The Drink takes You

"First you take a drink, then the drink takes a drink, then the drink takes you."
  - F. Scott Fitzgerald

First you write a character, then the character tells his story, then you take the credit.

For a Man to Write Fiction

"A woman must have money and room of her own if she is to write fiction."
  - Virginia Woolf

For a man to write fiction he needs desire, discipline, money and, of course, a woman to love. Without the woman, his life is his fiction.

Sell Out

"Writers are always selling somebody out."
  - Joan Didion

Sell out your hero and sell out your readers. Sell out your antagonist and sell out your books

Trust Inspiration

"When I sit at my table to write, I never know what it's going to be until I'm under way. I trust in inspiration, which sometimes comes and sometimes doesn't. But I don't sit back waiting for it. I work every day."
  - Alberto Moravia

Try it. Write every day. You will discover writing, and inspiration will discover you. You will learn you can trust it. Inspiration always comes every time. But writers beware! Inspiration will always out wait your complacency.

Television's Whore

"Television has raised writing to a new low."
  - Samuel Goldwyn

Television affects writing like a half rack of beer. It lightens her mood, loosens her tongue, slurs her speech, and removes her inhibitions. Instead of a lover, though, television is a pimp making writing his whore.

Two Word Quotations

"Two word quotations require two hundred words of thought."
  - S.R. Lundin

Quoting Gloria

"Writing is the only thing that, when I do it, I don't feel I should be doing something else."
  - Gloria Steinem

Writing is the only reason I could ever quote Gloria Steinem.

New Thing, New Way

"The secret of good writing is to say an old thing in a new way or to say a new thing in an old way."
  - Richard Harding Davis

Say an old thing in a new way for your father, a new thing in an old way for your grandfather, and a new thing in a new way forever.

Familiar to Us

"If a reporter doesn't like the person he's writing about, it shows up in his article."
  - Willie Stargell

Novelists draw from such a large group of unlikable acquaintances that they never use just one in their writings. Instead, they combine the worst of each into a single character and call the monster, Antagonist. There's no wonder why such characters seem so real to us. Most are.

Just the Lie

"Nowadays three witty turns of phrase and a lie make a writer."
  - G. C. Lichtenberg

Ah, the good old days: So innocent. Today, it's three lies for one witty turn, and the witty turn is optional.

Sincere Plagiarism

"Observe, don't imitate."
  - John M. Ford

Imitation is sincere plagiarism, like borrowing is sincere stealing.

Determination Writes the Novel

While research writes the paper and emotions write the poetry, determination writes the novel.
  - S.R. Lundin

Passion Creates

Passion creates the writer.
  - S.R. Lundin

Stop Writing

Stop writing, start dying? Maybe, but it smacks of beginner's belief. So what really happens when a writer quits writing? May you never know.
  - S.R. Lundin

Guts of a Writer

"Talent is helpful in writing, but guts are absolutely essential."
  - Jessamyn West

Discipline, persistence, patience, endurance -- the guts of a writer.

Live Present Tense

"Live in each season as it passes; breathe the air, drink the drink, taste the fruit."
  - Henry David Thoreau

Change season to present in the above quotation, and Thoreau gives excellent advice to writers. Live, breathe, drink, taste, and see: Be present in the present tense.

Mere Habit

"The mere habit of writing, of constantly keeping at it, of never giving up, ultimately teaches you how to write."
    - Gabriel Fielding

If habit is not the greatest teacher, it's easily the most inspirational.

A Reason

"Life is a tragedy for those who feel, and a comedy for those who think."
    - La Bruyere

Life is not a genre for those who write. It's a reason.

Prices to Pay

"You must want to enough. Enough to take all the rejections, enough to pay the price of disappointment and discouragement while you are learning. Like any other artist, you are learning your craft- then you can add all the genius you like."
    - Phyllis Whitney

Rejection, disappointment, and discouragement are small prices to pay when you're pursuing a passion.

First is The Heart

"The last thing one settles in writing a book is what one should put in first."
    - Pascal

The first thing one settles in writing a book is his heart.

Reward of Achievement

"To avoid criticism, do nothing, say nothing, be nothing."
    - Elbert Hubbard

Criticism is a reward of achievement.

Learning to Write

"Writing has laws of perspective, of light and shade just as painting does, or music. If you are born knowing them, fine. If not, learn them. Then rearrange the rules to suit yourself."
    - Truman Capote

Beware that you do not spend so much time learning how to write that you never write.

Equal Excitement

"Sure, it's simple, writing for kids… Just as simple as bringing them up."
   - Ursula K. LeGuin

It's an equal excitement, sending a child off to college and a book off to production... just as equal as the disappoint felt when either returns rejected.

Love What You Do

If you write every day with something to say, you'll love what you do and not throw it away.
   - S.R. Lundin

Day Without Writing

A day without writing is like a day without family.
   - S.R. Lundin

To Be Done

To be done writing is to be done living.
   - S.R. Lundin

Shortening Your Screenplay

Shortening your screenplay is like selling your possessions. You save the best for last.
  - S.R. Lundin

End of Editing

Publication: The end of editing; the beginning of revision.
  - S.R. Lundin

Don't Listen to Writers

"If I had to give young writers advice, I would say don't listen to writers talking about writing or themselves."
  - Lillian Hellman

Had I followed Lillian Hellman's advice, I never would have read her quotation. Unfortunately, though, when I first studied to write my first novel, I did so by listening to everyone with a voice. One adviser told me to hate adjectives. Another said I should never use semicolons. I was told to prefer short sentences, make my sentences longer, never use internal dialog because I could not possibly know the mind of another. I was instructed to make greater use of comma splices, remove the frame I put around my first novel, write like I talk (I like this advice), do this, do that, and "show" instead of "tell" a story.

"They," that elusive group of writing experts to whom I listened, spoke with the authority of having been published. They make me want to brush my teeth. I wasted too much time.

Young writers: Ms. Hellman's advice is solid. My contribution is unoriginal. If your goal is to become a writer, then pursue your passion, never forget Lillian's advice, and write, write, write.

Fiction Has to Make Sense?

"The difference between fiction and reality? Fiction has to make sense."
  - Tom Clancy

And for fiction to make sense, an author must write like a reader.

The Neck Rules Supreme

"Only in men's imagination does every truth find an effective and undeniable existence. Imagination, not invention, is the supreme master of art as of life."
  - Joseph Conrad

Conrad; leave it to him to speak with such an undeniable voice that, whatever his words, they simply must be true. And yet, less than one hundred years following his death, when the measure of a man includes the weight of his wallet, invention --not art--

has proven to be the supreme master of life. Just ask the man named Gates. Even though invention has usurped imagination as the supreme master of life, nothing has changed. Not really. Listen to Conrad say it, "Only in men's imagination does every truth find an effective and undeniable existence."

So let invention be the head, its enough that imagination is the neck that turns him at her will.

Tell It All

"No tale tells all."
  - Alexei Panshin

Your untold story can far exceed that which is told. Yours might have you losing something important, like your job, marriage, or health, but so what? Those are just tales. Excluding your death and a passion for finishing your story, keep writing. Your life is your story. Alexei Panshin was, of course, referring more to the written than to the human condition, but his quotation is fat with truth. No tale tells all? That's great! Form the excerpts of your life into the story you want to write. Even if you tell it all, half of your readers won't notice and the rest won't care.

Write for yourself.

Take it like a Lamppost

"Asking a working writer what he thinks about critics is like asking a lamppost how it feels about dogs."
- Christopher Hampton

On its surface, this quotation is funny. In an attempt to discover the source of the humor, I began by examining the simile. Where Hampton equated a working writer to a lamppost, the living to an inanimate, the reasoning to the illuminating, I found nothing funny about a writer sitting and writing like a lamppost standing and lighting. The humorless bores. I next considered Hampton's setting a critic equal to a dog. That is funny, but that sort of humor is as cheap and easy as a mother-in-law joke.

Christopher Hampton's pen is not that common. I was left with the naked source of humor in Hampton's quotation. His implied but not stated simile became: critics urinate on writers like dogs on lampposts. I hated the image. It went too far. I quickly returned to the beginning, reread the quote as a quote, recovered my grin from my frown, and resolved to avoid searching beyond the simple.

When criticism comes, I decided, I'll just take it like a lamppost.

The Prerequisites

"Beginning writers must appreciate the prerequisites if they hope to become writers. You pay your dues - which takes years."
  - Alex Haley

In this, my fourth year of writing seven days each week, I am beginning to understand and appreciate the wisdom in Alex Haley's words. Whereas the tendency of a beginning writer is to appreciate that he has written, the truth is his writings are like the first tries of a baby. From scribbling and tracing, he forms letters from naked imagination, sentences from the passions of his growing years, paragraphs in school, chapters out of experience and, finally, a whole book out of his life. Only then does the beginning writer appreciate both the prerequisites and the chasm that remains between his hope for his work and the reality of its failings. Only by paying his dues does a beginning writer mature into a real writer. Unfortunately, the dues are more than most will pay.

The Passion to Alter

"No passion in the world is equal to the passion to alter someone else's draft."
  - William Shakespeare

What are you writing? I once answered the question every time it was asked of me. Writing was new back then, so I answered with the engaging, enthusiastic, and unrestrained blabber of an idiot. I spoke as though I was on a mixture of speed and truth serum, but I was wrong to speak so freely. To this day, I regret taking too long to recognize that every time I told someone about my ideas, plot points, themes, characters, or anything else that I was writing, I would change it all the next morning. Inevitably, I was told to change this, revise that, go this way, make it happy, kill them all, explore love, blame God, and on-and-on.

At the end of a day, so many people had been so insistent about their little recommendations that I felt a subconscious pressure to comply with their demands. Unfortunately, I was born weak to the desire to please. Back then, I wrote like a Senator, restating positions, changing directions, disguising my actions, crafting slippery sentences, and revising my manuscript to please a majority of the constituents. It was not until I stopped talking that I was able to start listening. What I heard was the clamor of passionate people who had the desire, but not the time, to write books of their own. Altering my draft allowed them to be writers by proxy. Shakespeare left us another timeless truth, but I suspect what he called a passion to alter someone else's draft was really his acknowledgment of a universal desire to write. It is fortunate, then, that those who can write, write, and those who cannot write have, at least, a way to believe that they can.

In this manner, excluding critics, everyone is a writer.

What Matters to You

"The act of writing is an act of optimism. You would not take the trouble to do it if you felt it didn't matter."
- Edward Albee

The less optimistic an author is about his writing, the less pessimistic he will be after being rejected by literary agents and the other gate keepers who discourage writers who write. It is foolish to write what matters to them. That path leads to writer's block and the end of your ambition.

Write instead what matters to you. That is how it works. It is only by writing that you become a real writer, and real writers write what matters to them. Eventually they will find you. If not optimistic, at least be patient.

A Damn Deep Wit

"Substitute 'damn' every time you're inclined to write 'very;' your editor will delete it and the writing will be just as it should be."
- Mark Twain

The spotlight of Twain's humor was never a steady circle of light. The edges vibrate with laughter. Every time I steady my grin, squint my eyes, and look like a deer to see what he saw, I glimpse a very deep wit, or as he would have it, I glimpse a damn deep wit.

Show Don't Tell

"Don't tell me the moon is shining; show me the glint of light on broken glass."
  - Anton Chekhov

Show don't tell is a common refrain of fiction writing teachers. "Instead of telling readers that a woman is angry," they tell their students, "show them." Have the woman slam her pumps hard on the brakes, make her car tires scrape loud on the concrete, let a drop of morning coffee splash hot from her cup, break her finger nail in a fight with the window, get her arm out in the rain, and lift the broken nail of her middle finger at the man she still loves. If they see it, readers will know she's angry. They will want to know what happens next, and then you can tell them.

All of Your Intelligence

"Bring all your intelligence to bear on your beginning."
  - Elizabeth Bowen

Writers who follow Elizabeth Bowen's advice will find that, in addition to giving themselves a shot at making a good first impression on readers, their stories will seem to write themselves. It is when writers reach the end, however, that they are glad they did not exhaust all of their intelligence on the beginning. Smart endings are as difficult as intelligent beginnings.

Landmarks of the Past

"Writers are the main landmarks of the past."
  - Edward G. Bulwer-Lytton

No. The lives of great men and women are the main landmarks of the past, and writers are never great unless they are dead.

Passion's Ease

"Writing isn't hard. It isn't any harder than ditch-digging."
  - Patrick Dennis

It is the passion of the doer that determines the difficulty of the doing. Passionate writers enjoy one of man's easiest, most enjoyable, and rewarding forms of work. Unfortunately, they just don't know it.

Prostitutes

"Writing is like prostitution. First you do it for love, and then for a few close friends, and then for money."
  - Moliere

Writing really is like prostitution. Writers do share themselves with whomever pays them, they numb themselves from reality while they work, agents pimp them out on the street, and only the best make the big money. Hmm. It's no wonder Hollywood portrays them as drunks, psychos, and addicts.

C.R.A.P.

"Be obscure clearly."
   - E.B. White

The king of clarity pushing obscurity? That's like a rapper singing country.

Watch and See
Read and watch, write and see.
   - S.R. Lundin

Proof to See
"Proofread carefully to see if you any words out."
   - Author Unknown

Or to see what extra words are hiding in in your writings.

99% of Stories
"The reason 99% of all stories written are not bought by editors is very simple. Editors never buy manuscripts that are left on the closet shelf at home."
   - John Campbell

Today's reason why 99% of all stories are not bought by editors is as simple as the old reason. Instead of writers leaving manuscripts sitting on closet shelves at home, they're sending them to literary agents. The result is the same; editors never buy what they never see.

Thankful for Poets

"I firmly believe every book was meant to be written."
  - Marchette Chute

Had Marchette Chute been a literary agent, her "every book was meant to be written" might have been "only a few books were meant to be written, and my job is to find them. Yours is not one."

Writers, be thankful for poets.

The Writing Magic

"When you start writing the magic comes when the characters seem to take on a life of their own and write the words for themselves."
  - Alice Hoffman

Writing takes hard work, not magic. When you're writing and your characters refuse to come to life, be thankful. They need you. They're just characters, but they have an awesome ability of bringing writers to life.

Write Now, Right Now

"Everything changes when you change."
  - Jim Rohn

Everything changes when you write. Don't wait to start. Sure you'll be older and wiser when you finally begin, but your voice will be that of a child. Write now, right now.

Neither Man nor God

"Neither man nor God is going to tell me what to write."
  - James T. Farrell

Damn right! You're the boss. What you write is yours alone. Hide it. That way no one will ever know you existed.

Writer's Bite

"All of a writer that matters is in the book or books. It is idiotic to be curious about the person."
  - Jean Rhys

What? Idiotic to care about the writer? Even though they're damn hard to catch, I want to see the spider that bites me.

Ridiculous Money

"Writing is the only profession where no one considers you ridiculous if you earn no money."
  - Jules Renard

Writing is just one way you can make ridiculous amounts of money. Gambling is another.

Acceptance and Rejection

"Writing is a struggle between presence and absence."
  - Lu Ji

Publication is a struggle between feelings of acceptance and rejection.

Writing Is

"While writing is a convenience of income, income is an inconvenience of writing."
  - S.R. Lundin

Fired by Reading

"Reading usually precedes writing and the impulse to write is almost always fired by reading. Reading, the love of reading, is what makes you dream of becoming a writer."
  - Susan Sontag

Susan Sontag described how writing happened to me. From Dr. Sues to S.E. Hinton, Dickens to Hemingway, Tolstoy and Dostoevsky to James and Lawrence, Hugo, Goldsmith, Mann, Cervantes, Fitzgerald, Conrad, Joyce, and on-and-on, on-and-on, on-and-on, reading fired my impulse to write. But I've watched movies without dreaming of becoming an actor, listened to music without dreaming of becoming a musician, and read books without dreaming of becoming a writer. The love of reading, instead of "mak[ing me] dream," made me do. That's how you become a writer: you write.

Pantings of Your Fingers

"Fill your paper with the breathings of your heart..."
  - William Wordsworth

Fill your life with the pantings of your fingers.

Great Sentences

Many write great stories. Few write great sentences.
  - S.R. Lundin

Respectable Excuse

"The profession of book-writing makes horse racing seem like a solid, stable business."
  - John Steinbeck

When money is your motive for writing fiction, lie and say that it's not. You'll have a respectable excuse for being so broke.

Therefore I Write

"I think, therefore I am."
  - René Descartes

I've written, therefore I write.

First Loves

"Little Red Riding Hood was my first love. I felt that if I could have married Little Red Riding Hood I should have known perfect bliss."

- Charles Dickens

Goldilocks would have been my first love, if it wasn't for those damn bears.

Master in Death

"We are all apprentices in a craft where no one ever becomes a master."

- Ernest Hemingway

Concerning writers, master is a synonym for dead.

Swing for the Fence

"If you're a singer you lose your voice. A baseball player loses his arm. A writer gets more knowledge, and if he's good, the older he gets, the better he writes."

- Mickey Spillane

Regardless of age and experience, writers should swing for the fence. That's how to hit a home run.

Actions of Men

"I have always thought the actions of men the best interpreters of their thoughts."
  - John Locke

I have always thought the desires of most men the limit of their action; they sit and they want. For those who keep standing, their desires become their achievements.

Blockhead

"No man but a blockhead ever wrote except for money."
  - Samuel Johnson

From the money I make from writing, it's a wonder I can lift my head.

Calling a Screenplay

Calling a screenplay a template is like calling sheet music an outline.
  - S.R. Lundin

Need Nerve

"You need a certain amount of nerve to be a writer."
  - Margaret Atwood

Thick skin is helpful too.

Kiss of Death

"A kiss that speaks volumes is seldom a first edition."
  - Clare Whiting

Writing without passion is a sure kiss of death.

Broyard's Either/or Writers

"Either a writer doesn't want to talk about his work, or he talks about it more than you want."
  - Anatole Broyard

After completing my first novel, I placed the thick manuscript in a box under a cabinet in my dining room. I was unsure what to do with it. The book-in-a-box seemed foreign in my day job life. It was as though my heart was inside that box and, by opening the lid, someone might see me, see through me, know my passion, and then dismiss me as a dreamer or label my work a cute little hobby. Back then, I would never talk about the book.

My wife likes to host frequent dinner parties, and so it was that she began, only occasionally at first, withdrawing the box, removing the lid, and showing the contents to whomever happened to be sharing our table. The first time she did this, I became an apologist and quickly re-lid and re-hid the box. What could I say? It was a book-in-a-box. It was all about me.

I soon became an example of what Anatole Broyard meant in the second part of his quotation about writers. I had to check myself whenever someone asked me about my writing. Rather than engaging in conversation, where my questions would come in a number equal to my answers, I went through a phase of nonstop talking about writing, how wonderful it was, its influence on someone living a day-job life, how light, color, conversation, emotion, eye contact, and a thousand other sensory perceptions revealed to me a richer world, and on-and-on. I could not shut up. Finally, there came a time when Broyard's "either or" of writers no longer worked for me. It is a time of peace—a time to shut up—and it feels like right now.

Nobody Told Me (part one)

"No tears in the writer, no tears in the reader."
  - Robert Frost

I remember the moment like it was just now. Two years ago, at about five-thirty in the morning, when the fire in my fireplace was failing after its morning rage, I had reached the critical point in my first novel where my hero had to die, and I had to kill him.

I suppose I knew it was coming all along, but I had not considered that the event would be anything more than a paragraph or two of well-crafted sentences. Thankfully, a subconscious emotion plucked my heart to warn me that something painful prowled at the tips of my fingers.

I was about to kill the man: my hero, the character I had spent nine months carefully developing into a young man who could be admired by all. Because I grew up without my father, I have never loved a man. It is a flaw of mine: I love no man. My hero? Well, he was different. I had created him in my image. I had taken great care to develop him into what I considered to be an ideal man. The emotion I felt that morning hurt my heart, so I stopped writing only long enough to add wood to my fire. I remembered childhood stories about Biblical fathers who had killed their sons. If a father could kill his son on earth, I reasoned, it would be nothing for me to kill a son on paper. The outside and inside of my house were still winter dark, my three children were still upstairs asleep, the damn cat was somewhere outside pawing a window but, when I returned to my writing desk, I thought of nothing but the task at hand. I went back into the world of my novel and killed him.

The simple act of killing my character cost me nothing more than a bit of mental innocence but, really, what is that? I felt sorry for the loss. I hurt for what my hero was and for what he could have been, but I did not cry. It was one sad day in my life but, from what those who have read the novel tell me, those eight or ten who cried and got mad at me for killing my hero, I wondered at Robert Frost's quotation. There had been no tears in the writer.

The fire ended, the kids woke up and went to school, I went to work, the cat did absolutely nothing, and I remember wondering if I had grown into a heartless man.

The answer came the following morning...

Surprises in the Writer

"No surprise in the writer, no surprise in the reader."
  - Robert Frost

...a continuation of Nobody Told Me: My wife brought to our marriage a signed, first edition copy of Where the Red Fern Grows, a story written by author Wilson Rawls. I read the book to my children back when they were somewhere between the ages of eight and ten. Each night for maybe a week or two, they would come upstairs, sit on my bed, play with our kitten, and listen while I read to them the story of a boy and his two dogs. At first, my son would secretly violate the personal space of one of the girls who, in turn, would violate my sanity by making frequent interruptions of my reading.

They started the book like a cold engine but, in time, the kids so warmed up to the tale that I believe each of them watched *Where the Red Fern Grows* like it was a movie playing in their minds. Wilson Rawls so captured their imaginations that my son stopped playing his tricks, the girls stopped watching for him, and the three united as protesters who bitterly opposed me everytime I said, "That's enough for tonight."

Anyone who has read the book can guess what happened when I read the end of the story. In my room, on my bed, me reading with a breathless voice, my wife and three children crying like they were separating for life, and my young family experiencing together the awful pain that readers feel when authors build and then kill their heroes. I thought forward in time to the day I would write a novel, and I vowed I would never kill the hero. Now move ahead in time to the morning following the one during which I claimed to kill the hero of my first novel. That next morning, I again had a blazing fire in the fireplace, the time was again early, the kids were now in their one year of alignment, when all three were in high school, the kitten was a plump, bossy cat, again pawing a window outside in the dark, and I was back at my writing desk aligning my words to my will.

Kill the hero? Hell no! I wanted to elevate him. I worked and reworked the story until I got it right. Nearly three weeks passed before the morning of the big surprise. I had been writing from about four that morning right up to the exact moment it happened. My daily fire had reduced to a glow from which maroon flames waved lambent arms, as though the fire was waving goodbye to my innocence. I was alone at my writing desk, and I was stunned. I did not even hear Lisa come into the room, but I heard her when she stopped behind where I sat with my face in my hands and my head drooped to the floor.

I could not look up.

"What's wrong?" she asked. "What's happened?"

From that moment on, I understood the accuracy and truth of Robert Frost's full quotation. "No tears in the writer, no tears in the reader. No surprise in the writer, no surprise in the reader." Without giving away the ending of *Shooting an Albatross*, I can say with conviction that Frost exposed me with his truths. Surprises? Oh yeah. Tears? I'll tell you what, you read the book and answer for yourself. All I will say is that Frost understood the soul of writers and their writing.

A Solitary Occupation

"Writing is a solitary occupation. Family, friends, and society are the natural enemies of the writer. He must be alone, uninterrupted, and slightly savage if he is to sustain and complete an undertaking."
  - Jessamyn West

At the root of Mary Jessamyn West's quotation is her notion that writers are strange. She paints a verbal picture of a loner, an enemy of society, friends, and family, and a person who must be savage. What is this beast? Of course writers work alone, but it is their involvement with family, friends, and society that sustains them—not isolated savagery. Writers need life. They need love and, most of all, writers need to remain fully engaged in society. If not, they certainly will become one of West's monsters. Just watch any of Hollywood's movies about writers.

Paperwork

"I love being a writer. What I can't stand is the paperwork."
  - Peter de Vries

A random sample of writer's desks includes little piles of paper. For some, the piles are huge. The papers include notes here-and-there, letters to put away whenever time permits, ideas scribbled on napkins, important letters to file (a few that remain inside opened envelopes), one or two email messages, a short, seventeen page print-out of some sort of research, a notepad, an assortment of loose business cards , three printed chapters of a current piece of work that is undergoing review, and that's just the desk.

There are, of course, those wads of paper on the floor around the waste basket.

Who's Afraid of Virginia Woolf?

"...talents of the novelist: ...observation of character, analysis of emotion, people's feelings, personal relations..."
  - Virginia Woolf

Virginia Woolf's quotation reminds me of an incident that occurred back when I was writing my first novel. I had been getting up to write at four a.m. for about one year at the time, but I had not yet acknowledged that the experience was affecting the way I looked at the world. Sure, I had already purchased a new camera and had taken pictures of everything that bloomed on my little two-acre property; that was unexpected, and I had already jumped to my feet and shouted "they're cheating" at my television screen after seeing a director using music, light, facial expressions, eye movements, and a thousand other cheats to influence his viewers the way I was trying to influence readers, and I had even started watching to find character in people.

Count Leo Tolstoy is said to have thought the eye of a writer focuses on the itty-bitty, but I was unaware of this weird little fact at the time of my doctor visit. My doctor was and still is Oregon's premier MS doctor, and I was and still am only one of his over one thousand patients.

On the day of my visit, he was standing at his desk, smiling, indicating that my wife and I should sit in the two black leather chairs positioned across from his desk, and he stared as I moved to take my seat. I knew he was watching, so I smiled and pretended I was not making a supreme effort to sit with the grace of a statesman.

My doctor was nearly seventy years old, so he probably saw through my effort. He wore a tie under his white doctor jacket, was serious about his work, and once told me he had committed his life to finding a cure for MS before he died. I never asked him why. He had gotten a medical degree from Georgetown University, another from a school in Chicago, an assortment of specialty certificates, and a Ph.D.

I remember thinking I could call him Doctor-Doctor because he was both a physician and a Ph.D. He might have noticed me grinning at the thought, but he asked about nothing but the progression of my illness. It is because my wife is a hospital pharmacist that Doctor-Doctor goes into greater detail with her than he does with me. The two speak in a hospital street slang that I find neither easy to understand nor interesting to hear, and so I often allow myself to listen to their conversation like a school boy listening to his mother talk with his teacher. That is exactly what I was doing when it happened.

In Virginia Woolf's quotation, she identified "observation of character, analysis of emotion, people's feelings, [and] personal relations" as the "talents of the novelist." I would never call what I did that day a talent, but it was definitely something like Tolstoy's look at the itty-bitty. While Doctor-Doctor looked at and talked to my pharmacist, I stared at him. I watched the movements of his eyes and hands, sought emotion from the width of his eye lids, tried to equate his emotions to the movement of his facial skin, turns of his head, leans forward and back in his chair, and from the volume of his voice, but I did so without listening to a single word he said. I sought the external manifestations of his internal feelings and emotions. I watched for his true character behind the facade of his profession.

I decided he was tired but willed himself against fatigue. I knew he was a grandfather, but I decided he treated his grandchildren like great-grandchildren. He worked all of the time, was in charge of every aspect of his life, and was intense with his grown children. I judged him to be so protected by respect that he was like a president in a grocery store; the common was beyond him.

While I watched, recorded, replayed, and searched to discover his character, I saw Doctor-Doctor express concern with his eyes. I followed his look to my pharmacist, found her looking as confused as he appeared to be, and I watched them both turn and stare at me. Doctor-Doctor repeated whatever he had already said to me.

"You're doing that thing again," my wife whispered. "You told me to tell you when it's happening. You said I should tell you to stay in the moment."

"Thank you," I said.

Today, I refer to that day at the doctor's office as my Virginia Woolf Day. The true talent of a novelist, I have decided, is not simply an ability to observe and to analyze, but it's the ability to do so while remaining sane in the moment. Who's afraid of Virginia Woolf? Not you. The sane stay in the moment.

Cold at the Core

"Every writer I know has trouble writing."
  - Joseph Heller

Most writers have little trouble writing. They can put words on paper for hours on end. Their problems come from their desire for readers. Writers without readers are like planets devoid of life, cold to the core, spinning in the dark, entirely alone. Even in this dystopia, they still feel the pull of something way out there, some sliver of light to which they are drawn like planets to a sun. In time, they actually become a part of that sun, and then don't they shine?

The great trouble with writing is a problem of patience.

Morally Illegal

"I'd rather be caught holding up a bank than stealing so much as a two-word phrase from another writer."
- Jack Smith

Insane! Why steal someone else's words? Who needs them?

True writers find their own words so deep in their minds that another's words are worthless. Not only is plagiarism morally illegal, those who commit it miss the great pleasures of writing: using their own words in their own voices, feeling and sharing the passions, fears, lusts and other emotions of their characters, finding new meaning for their lives, turning their wants into needs, and then into talents, adding their own sentences to the unfinished novel of human understanding, and on-and-on, on-and-on, on-and-on...

Tax Slush Pile

"Query letters are like tax payments to the income tax slush pile. Both get answered by form letter, might result in audit, and are sent with the hope for income, but they also carry a poison capable of depressing your greatest ambitions. Writers be thankful queries cannot land you in jail."

- S.R. Lundin

Bottle Sucking Schizophrenics

"Writers aren't exactly people.... they're a whole bunch of people trying to be one person."

- F. Scott Fitzgerald

Fiction writers need the public to buy their books, but they do not need the public's desire for strange writers. Be alone with your imagination, see the silent, feel the emotions of your characters, cry if you must, laugh when you're alone, but resist the charm and allure of becoming one of Hollywood's frazzled, disheveled, suicidal, chain smoking, bottle sucking schizophrenics. There are enough of those.

Writers have a whole bunch of people telling them who they should be, but beware! These people are not fictional characters; they're real.

Hollywood wants writers to fit a stereotype.

Lessing's Law for the Novel

"There are no laws for the novel. There never have been, nor can there ever be."
  - Doris Lessing

Lessing's Law for the Novel: *There are no laws for the novel*
  Corollary 1: *There never have been*
  Corollary 2: *There never can be*

Doris Lessing's circular logic and ironical proof achieve a rare height of elegance. I suspect, however, there's not a writer alive who will obey the law.

Cultivating Their Cud

"Any writer, I suppose, feels that the world into which he was born is nothing less than a conspiracy against the cultivation of his talent."
  - James Baldwin

Writers work alone. They wonder alone, imagine alone, and create alone, but then they submit finished writings to the judgment of the critical world. While writers expect to hear "bravo!" they more often hear "no-go!" They should not let it bring them down. Criticism is not a conspiracy.

It's just the sound critics make when cultivating their cud.

No Refunds for Skipping

"I try to leave out the parts that people skip."
  - Elmore Leonard

What is read today, though skipped last year, gets honored next month. Fickle fellows favor fashion, though astute authors are always audacious; they keep their pennies. They refund nothing for the parts readers skip.

Cridiots

"There is no mistaking the dismay on the face of a writer who has just heard that his brain child is a deformed idiot."
  - L. Sprague de Camp

Excepting, of course, the professional opinions of deformed cridiots (critics who are idiots).

Voodoo Word Game

"In composing, as a general rule, run a pen through every other word you have written; you have no idea what vigor it will give your style."
- Sydney Smith

I played Smith's game with a simple sentence:
___ advice ___ helps ___ write ___, but ___ you __ read ___ crap?

Instead of adding vigor to my writing style, the exercise spoke a truth and asked a question. I won't play that again. What if these hidden communications had been "writing will kill you" or "today you will die?" Smith's voodoo game of words needs a warning label. Write at your own risk.

Ultimate Fighting

"Listening to critics is like letting Muhammad Ali decide which astronaut goes to the moon."
- Robert Duvall

Challenging critics is like taking on a young Muhammad Ali. While he had muscle and moves long ago, critics have them today, and they never use gloves. There's no wonder ultimate fighting has grown in popularity! It's how writers meet their critics.

Writing is Work

Writing is work without pay and a boss.
  - S.R. Lundin

Challenge for Fiction Writers

"The skill of writing is to create a context in which other people can think."
  - Edwin Schlossberg

The challenge for fiction writers is creating scenes readers can see, emotions they can feel, and thoughts they must think.

Wonder

"We don't write what we know. We write what we wonder about."
  - Richard Peck

I know the world is full of wonder, so what was Peck saying?

Don't be Fooled

"Write your first draft with your heart. Re-write with your head."
  - From the movie Finding Forrester

Don't be fooled. Do the opposite. If you write the first draft with your head and re-write with your heart, you will take months off the time it takes to finish your masterpiece.

The Medicine Man of Mayo

"If you write one story, it may be bad; if you write a hundred, you have the odds in your favor."
- Edgar Rice Burroughs

For a season back in the time I call B.C. (Before Cane), I would travel to the Mayo Clinic in Scottsdale, Arizona to see Dr. Jonathan Carter. Whether I read, said, or simply thought of his name, I would always get this little grin on my face because the doctor's name caused me to think of Edgar Rice Burroughs.

Burroughs was a prolific writer in the first half of the 1900s who preferred writing series of books over writing stand-alone stories. While he is best known for his *Tarzan of the Apes* series, it was his John Carter, Warlord of Mars (1918), series that had me smiling on my visits to the hospital in the desert. Back then, I made the mistake of imputing the fictional abilities of John Carter on Dr. Jonathan Carter. I expected Dr. Carter to give me a miracle drug, enter me in a double-blind, triple-success Mayo Clinic study, possess the secret for halting the progression of my illness, guarantee I would not be in a wheelchair before I was forty, help me, save me, solve world hunger, and on-and-on.

While John Carter, the Warlord of Mars, could have done so, Dr. Carter, the Medicine Man of Mayo, could not. These experiences with fiction and medicine left me addicted to the medicine of fiction, but it is in this regard I am healed. While writing, I discovered, there is no illness. Edgar Rice Burroughs proved the point of his quotation with his work. He wrote so many stories in his life that, in doing so, he forced the odds of success in his favor. While Burroughs provides an excellent example for writers seeking the eventual success of their stories, his advice gives greater hope to writers seeking nothing more than the success of life.

Flinging Horse Excrement

"If a book is not alive in the writer's mind, it is as dead as year-old horse-shit."
    - Stephen King

Looking out of the window where I write, I can see the field in which our horses do their business, the two horses, their heads bent and stomachs fattening on the spring grass that grows faster than weeds at this time of the year, and I can see one of the greens of the golf course that borders my little place.

I sometimes sit out on my porch swing and watch the golfers as they pass, but it is when a golfer slices his ball into the horse pasture that I pay close attention. I stop reading, glance to the field, grin, and watch to see what happens next. The golfers always stop at the electric fence. They stand unmoving, look left and right, and search for a particular ball among all of the other white balls and fresh brown piles. I know what they're thinking. They usually say something to the others in their party that I wish I could hear. It just has to be funny. A golfer will point his club at something in the field, turn his head back-and-forth, throw his hand like a wet rag, and walk away to where his friends are watching, waiting, and laughing. Because the reward of golf balls exceeds the risk of stepping in horse manure, I collcted them, but I used my son rather than collect them myself.

When he was young, My son would take a bucket and charge the field like an Easter egg hunt. He maneuvered the fresh piles, collected the golf balls, and returned home as proud as a dog. For me, it was a sweet deal He always washed them, threw out the balls that were damaged, and sorted the good ones by both quality and logo. Time flattens the solid waste excrement of horses. Both the weather and horse hooves cause the lumps to become so hard that they take on the properties of Frisbees. My son discovered this just before he discovered his mother's disapproval of his game of flinging the hard, dry, and dead disks of dung. Because Stephen King equates books that are not alive in writers' minds to year-old horse manure, I imagine I know what he means. I can see it.

Instead of horse-shit and my son, though, I imagine readers maneuvering fields of golf balls and flinging hard, flat, dead, and crappy books. I can even picture readers shoveling piles of such books as they come fresh off the press.

Newlove

"Remember: Writing can get you fed to a lion whose teeth draw your whole face into its foul wet breath and cut your skull with knives. There's no soft way to put this. A black hole swallows you up. Willpower's no help. Getting in print is like beating cancer but losing a lung, staying in print is hopeless. Your best work goes begging.....Today's paragraph comes, a word from the heart of the universe, and shines in the darkness, unquenched. And you ask for power, wisdom, and love as you make the anvil sing."

- Donald Newlove

Whew! What ever happened to the old love?

Master Mind

"I am a galley slave to pen and ink."

- Honore de Balzac

Master is in the mind.

6 | STEPPING STONES

My son, Steven, surprised me one father's day. He had me keep my eyes closed while he led me out to where my wife and his sisters stood waiting and watching.

"No peeking," they kept repeating.

Steven positioned me on our patio, told me to look, and said, "Happy Father's Day.

What a surprise!

Steven had cut circles from a plastic bucket, poured three concrete stepping stones in the circles, selected

125

three writing quotations, had them engraved on plaques, and he had mounted the plaques on the stones. My commitment to learning how to write and to writing every day had been so personal to me that I had missed one of writing's greatest lesson: No one writes alone. I hadn't noticed Steven was watching.

If you are an unknown writer who loves to write, keep going. Even if the world never takes notice, those who love you will. The reward is more than enough.

Staring out of windows

"What no wife of a writer can ever understand is that a writer is working when he's staring out the window."
  - Burton Rascoe

This is the first of the three quotations my son had given to me for Father's Day. I placed all three stepping sones out where I could see them everytime I barbecue.

Stepping Stone One

What a treat Rasco's quote is to read. Every time I read it, I laugh. The words he used, though simple enough, bring to mind James Thurber's character, Walter Mitty (from The Secret Life of Walter Mitty). Poor Mitty, poor Rascoe, but what about all of those wives with husbands staring out of windows?

One with the earth

"How vain it is to sit down to write when you have not stood up to live."
- Henry David Thoreau

This is a second quotation my son had engraved on a plate that he affixed to a stepping stone outside where I barbecue. Why does Thoreau's quotation trouble me?

Rather than stare at it, I read the words from a corner of my eye, looking more like an embarrassed dog than a man awed by the profound. Am I convicted? Is it vanity? My picture of Mr. Thoreau is not one of him floating out on the Pond under a warm and buzzing sky but, instead, I see him laying on the ground, doing nothing but feeling, and discovering his destiny of becoming one with the earth, of becoming something like a pumpkin left in the field one month after harvest.

But then what did Thoreau do?

Thoreau stood up to live, sat down to write and, in so doing, left the quotation that lives at my feet. I have never given respect to Thoreau's Bohemian style, and I've always shied away from Thoreau to gaze at Emerson. Emerson, though, circles me back to Thoreau.

What a mess--especially at this time in my life when I am forced to sit down to live.

Stepping Stone Two

How vain it is to sit down
and write when you have
not stood up to live.

- Henry David Thoreau

Ubiquitous and Invisible

"An author in his book must be like God in the universe, present everywhere and visible nowhere."
  - Gustave Flaubert

This is the third of the three quotations my son placed on stepping stones near my barbecue, and it is, by far, the most interesting to me. First, Flaubert. I took his novel, Madame Bovary, with me on vacation in Mexico. About eight years ago, I was sitting under a palapa in Puerto Vallarta, reading an unwieldy, leather-bound copy of the book, wondering about the effects of sand on archival quality paper, when I encountered Flaubert's sense of humor.

The main character of Flaubert's story was a ruran man— a doctor —who referred to his wife's feet as "two cold stones at the end of the bed." Because I remember the metaphor and still laugh at the image, though I've read nothing else by Flaubert, I like him. As for his quotation about an author in his book, I have mixed feelings. I of course appreciate Flaubert's truth, but what of this elevated comparison of an author to the God of the universe? I wonder at a tone of arrogance, but if a story is a universe and its author a creator, then Gustave said it well.

Ubiquitous and invisible, writers write.

Stepping Stone Three

APPENDIX A | LIST OF PILLARS

Scott Adams

Brian Adiss

Edward Albee

Margaret Anderson

Maxwell Anderson

Anonymous

Merit Antares

Sholem Asch

Isaac Asimov

Margaret Atwood

Walter Bagehot

Russell Baker

James Baldwin

Honore de Balzac

Bill Barnes

Hilaire Belloc

Jorge Luis Borges

C. N. Bovee

Catherine Drinker Bowen

Elizabeth Bowen

Ray Bradbury

Dorthea Brande

Justice Brandeis

Gerald Brenan

David Brin

Anatole Broyard

La Bruyere

Pearl S. Buck

Edward G. Bulwer-Lytton

Anthony Burgess

Edgar Rice Burroughs

Michel Butor

Robert Byrne

Lord Byron

L. Sprague de Camp

John Campbell

Elias Canetti

Truman Capote

Orson Scott Card

Liz Carpenter

Jeffery A. Carver

Miguel de Cervantes

Raymnd Chandler

Anton Chekhov

C. J. Cherryh

Gilbert K. Chesterton

Agatha Christie

Marchette Chute

Tom Clancy

Samuel Taylor Coleridge

Cyril Connolly

Joseph Conrad

Michael Crichton

Walter Cronkite

Richard Harding Davis

Inigo de Leon

Patrick Dennis

René Descartes

Charles Dickens

Allyson Dickey

Joan Didion

Benjamin Disraeli

E. L. Doctorow

Robert Duvall

Albert Einstein

T. S. Eliot

Stanley Elkin

Harlan Ellison

Ralph Waldo Emerson

James T. Farrell

William Faulkner

Edna Ferber

Gabriel Fielding

Finding Forrester (the movie)

F. Scott Fitzgerald

Gustave Flaubert

John M. Ford

John Fowles

Robert Frost

Carlos Fuentes

William Gass

Samuel Goldwyn

Baltasar Gracián

Alex Haley	Aldous Huxley
Donald Hall	Lu Ji
Christopher Hampton	Samuel Johnson
Peter Handke	Lawrence Kasdan
L. P. Hartley	Stephen King
Anthony Hope Hawkins	Henriette Anne Klauser
Nathaniel Hawthorne	Philip Larkin
Melinda Haynes	Stainislaw J. Lec
William Hazlitt	Ursula K. LeGuin
William Hefferman	John Lennon
Robert Heinlein	Elmore Leonard
Joseph Heller	Doris Lessing
Lillian Hellman	G. C. Lichtenberg
Ernest Hemingway	Gordon Lish
Alice Hoffman	John Locke
Julia Ward Howe	Jack London
Elbert Hubbard	Longfellow
Victor Hugo	Samuel Lover

Norman Mailer	Norbet Platt
Bernard Malamud	Enrique Jardiel Poncela
Jef Mallett	Katherine Anne Porter
Thomas Mann	Ayn Rand
W. Somerset Maugham	Robert Rankin
James Michener	Burton Rascoe
Moliere	Jules Renard
Tirso de Molina	Jean Rhys
Alberto Moravia	Jim Rohn
Christopher Morley	Leo Rosten
Pete Murphy	William Saroyan
Donald Newlove	John Scalzi
Larry Niven	Edwin Schlossberg
Sharon O'Brien	William Shakespeare
George Orwell	George Bernard Shaw
Alexei Panshin	Sidney Sheldon
Blaise Pascal	Jack Smith
Richard Peck	Logan Pearsall Smith

Sydney Smith

Susan Sontag

Mickey Spillane

Willie Stargell

John Steinbeck

Gloria Steinem

Gwen Stephani

Peggy Teeters

Henry David Thoreau

Leo Tolstoy

Mark Twain

Mary Heaton Vorse

Peter de Vries

Lawrence Welk

Jessamyn West

E. B. White

Clare Whiting

APPENDIX B | SOURCE LIST

While there are hundreds of public domain Websites with, literally, thousands of quotations about everything to do with writers and writing, any source list will be out of date the same day it's printed. Many will have little errors impossible to find.

Still, the following is a partial list of the Websites from which I discovered a treasure trove of writing quotations:

BookorBust – Inspirational Quotes – For Writers Only
http://bookorbust.blogspot.com/2011/07/inspirational-quotes-for-writers-only.html

Proverbia.net - Writers
http://en.proverbia.net/citastema.asp?tematica=1323

Ghostwriter Dad 50 Inspirational Writing Quotes
http://ghostwriterdad.com/50-inspirational-writing-quotes/

Eminent Quotables: What Writers Say About Writing
http://grammar.ccc.commnet.edu/grammar/quotes/quotes_frames.htm

Inspirational Writing Quotes
http://kindredheartwriters.com/2011/02/inspirational-writing-quotes.html

Quotes about Writing
http://koti.mbnet.fi/pasenka/quotes/q-writ.htm
Inspirational Quotes about Writing by Writers 76
http://russbaleson.hubpages.com/hub/Inspirational-

Quotes-On-Writing-By-Writers - 20 Inspiring Quotes to Help You Finish Writing Your Book... This Year
http://samhornpop.wordpress.com/2010/01/06/20-inspiring-quotes-to-help-you-finish-writing-your-book-this-year/

Inspirational quotes for writers
http://scriptlarva.wordpress.com/inspiration-for-writers/

Thinkexist.com
http://thinkexist.com/quotations/writing/

50 Best Inspiring Quotes for Writers
http://voices.yahoo.com/20-best-inspiring-quotes-writers-286777.html

The Write Quotes – Quotes about Writers and Writing
http://www.angelfire.com/al/thewritesite/quotes.html

Be a Better Writer – Creative Writing Quotes
http://www.be-a-better-writer.com/creative-writing-quotes.html

Writing for Children Workshops – Writing Quotes
http://www.bethanyroberts.com/writing_quotes.htm

Brainy Quote™
http://www.brainyquote.com/quotes/keywords/write.html

Change The World With Words – Forty Inspirational Quotes for Writers
http://www.changetheworldwithwords.com/forty-inspirational-quotes-for-writers/

Fiction Writers' Mentor – Inspirational Writing Quotes
http://www.fiction-writers-mentor.com/inspirational-writing-quotes.html

Ink Think writing quotes
http://www.fontayne.com/ink/quotewrite.html

Quotes about Writing
http://www.goodreads.com/quotes/tag/writing

Quotes about Writing
http://www.hearttouchers.com/writer_s_quotes

Inspirational Quotes – a great collection of writing quotes
http://www.inspirational-quotes.info/writing.html

Inspirational Quotes – Quotes for Writers
http://www.inspirational-
quotes.us/quotes_for_writers.php

Musings of a Novelista
http://www.karen-strong.com/2009/08/28/inspirational-
writing-quotes/

Quotable Quotes on Writers and Writing
http://www.logicalcreativity.com/jon/quotes.html
Inspirational Writing Quotes: Words of Wisdom by

Published Writers
http://www.love-quotes-and-
quotations.com/inspirational-writing-quotes.html

Motivational and Inspirational Quotes about Writing
http://www.motivational-inspirational-
corner.com/getquote.html?categoryid=96

nsrider.com - Writing quotes
http://www.nsrider.com/quotes/writing.htm

The Quote Garden
http://www.quotegarden.com/writing.html

Inspirational Quotes for Writers
http://www.shellistevens.com/inspirational-quotes-for-
writers/

Quotes of Inspiration for Writers
http://www.squidoo.com/quotes-of-inspiration-for-writers

A Showcase of Inspirational Writing Quotes
http://www.winepressofwords.com/2011/01/a-showcase-of-inspirational-writing-quotes/

Write Attitude - Inspirational Quotes (focus is not on writing)
http://www.writeattitude.net/quotes.php

WritersServices Quotes from Writers
http://www.writersservices.com/mag/m_quotes_writers.htm

Quotes assembled by Amberdine
https://sites.google.com/site/amberdine/beginning

Quoteland.com - Authors & Writing
http://www.quoteland.com/topic/Authors-Writing-Quotes/14/

Nebraska Center for Writers - Quotations for Writers
http://mockingbird.creighton.edu/ncw/quotes.htm

Writer's Remorse - Quotations: Writers on Writing
http://writersremorse.com/news/quotations-writers-writing

Famous Writers Quotes
http://judithpordon.tripod.com/poetry/famous_writers_quotes.html

ABOUT THE AUTHOR

Steven Lundin won 2009 Independent Novel Award for his first novel, *Shooting an Albatross*, after which time he completed an unpublished sequel, earned a screenwriting certificate from the New York Film Academy, finished six feature-length screenplays, and devoted several years to collecting and studying quotations about writing.

Lundin holds an MBA and actuarial enrollment. He is seventeen year vice-president, marketing director, and co-owner of a foundation engineering company.

Lundin lives and writes in Hillsboro, Oregon.

WRITINGS BY STEVEN R. LUNDIN

BOOKS

Shooting an Albatross

Peeking at Pillars

SCREENPLAYS

Shooting an Albatross

Legacy Management

Border Clash

Relapse

Jawheads

Downpour

www.ingramcontent.com/pod-product-compliance
Lightning Source LLC
Chambersburg PA
CBHW061304280526
45784CB00002B/883

* 9 7 8 1 4 7 0 0 3 4 0 7 8 *